WITH UNBLEST FEET

A Journey to Asia's Holy Mountains

IAIN CAMPBELL

Dundas Press

Copyright © 2017 by Iain Campbell

All rights reserved. This book or any portion thereof may not be reproduced or used in any manner whatsoever without the express written permission of the publisher except for the use of brief quotations in a book review or scholarly journal.

First Printing: 2017

ISBN-13: 978-1546647096

Cover design by adamhaystudio.com

Published By Dundas Press

www.dundaspress.com

To my parents

Accompanying photographs can be viewed at this website:
www.dundaspress.com/with-unblest-feet

CONTENTS

	Prologue	Pg 2
1	Emei Shan	Pg 10
2	Lhasa	Pg 31
3	To Kailash	Pg 48
4	The Kora	Pg 56
5	West	Pg 76
6	Aksai Chin	Pg 84
7	To Kashgar	Pg 101
8	Taklamakan	Pg 119
9	To Kygyzstan	Pg 133
10	North	Pg 149
11	Iran	Pg 173
12	Chak Chak	Pg 181
13	Ararat	Pg 197
	Epilogue	Pg 212

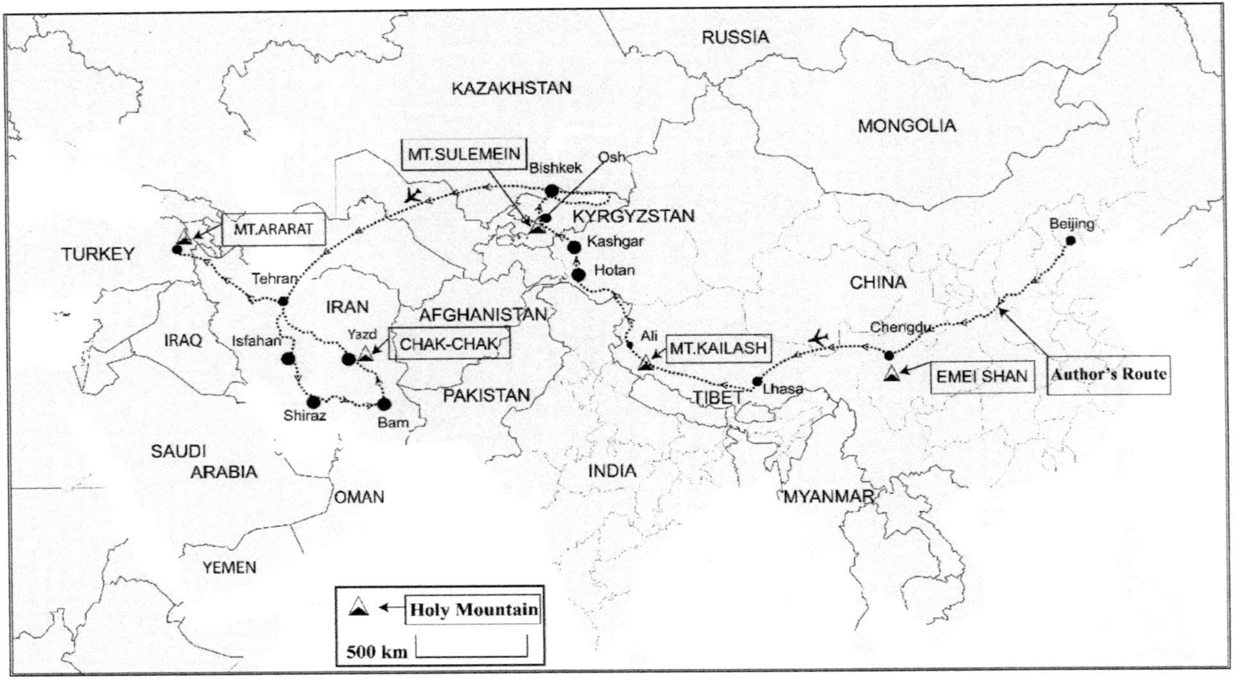
RUSSIA
KAZAKHSTAN
MONGOLIA
MT.SULEMEIN
Bishkek
Osh
KYRGYZSTAN
Kashgar
Hotan
MT.ARARAT
TURKEY
Tehran
IRAN
AFGHANISTAN
IRAQ
Isfahan
Yazd
CHAK-CHAK
Shiraz
Bam
PAKISTAN
SAUDI
ARABIA
OMAN
YEMEN
INDIA
Ali
MT.KAILASH
TIBET
Lhasa
MYANMAR
CHINA
Beijing
Chengdu
EMEI SHAN
Author's Route
Holy Mountain
500 km

PROLOGUE

A monk was sitting on the steps of the prayer hall in a sleeveless maroon tunic and trainers. Beside him, a cork-stoppered thermos flask with a folded chapatti balanced on top of it.

"You have walked here?"

"Yes."

I had walked for a week from Leh, the capital of Ladakh, along the Zanskar valley to reach his monastery. He poured me thick, yellow tea. The leaves did not sink in my bowl, but stayed suspended in the syrup of hot milk and sugar. He slurped his, straining it through teeth the same colour.

"I have walked here too, many years ago. I have walked from Tibet." His eyes stared at me, searching and enlarged by the distorting lenses of his spectacles. The skin on his bare arms was flecked with liver spots and creased as though it had been left folded in the sun too long.

Throughout India there are groups of Tibetan exiles like him, part of the exodus of Buddhist monks from Tibet to India fleeing the Cultural Revolution. They are concentrated in the more mountainous regions where the climate is similar to what they have left behind: the foothills of Himachal Pradesh, the hill-stations of West Bengal, the ghats of Karnataka.

They had settled in large numbers in Ladakh. Although Indian territory, Ladakh is geographically and ethnographically an extension of the Tibetan plateau. The land is dry and treeless, sheltered from the monsoon by the Himalayas. The people are ethnically Mongol; they farm barley, sheep, and yak, and they are Buddhist. The Tibetan border is only one hundred kilometres away from the capital, Leh.

"Come, I want to show you."

He led me into a dark hall where the air was sweet with the smell of incense and butter. My eyes slowly adjusted to the darkness and I could see rows of low benches arranged around the centre of the hall. The raised dais at one end was dominated by a giant Buddha looking into middle distance with almond shaped eyes, holding between his fingers an opaque cobweb of silk scarves that had been cast to him as offerings. At his crossed legs were crumpled rupee notes tucked under small rocks or piles of rice. Lined up in ranks on either side were smaller statues of lesser deities and at the end of the platform an incongruous stack of red thermos flasks looking as if they were recent additions to the Buddhist pantheon.

He beckoned me over to a dark wooden cupboard whose handles were worn and polished by decades of fingers and palms and took out some painted scrolls, "mandalas." Unrolled one at a time the material opened to display cracks like the skin on his shoulders.

"These ones I bring with me. From my monastery, so that they are not burnt." That was all he said about his flight from Tibet. He did not mention the traumas of that terrible period four decades earlier; the courtyards of monasteries running with blood; the monks being forced at gunpoint to rape nuns from their sister orders. He did not talk about the journey either, across the desolate plateau; the high passes to India; the dry wind and the sun. Only "I walked from Tibet ... I took them with me so they would not be burnt."

His fingers stroked the three mandalas. I cannot remember what the first and the last one showed, but the middle one I remember clearly. It was a map of the universe; a diagrammatic representation of the mountain ranges and oceans that make up the Buddhist cosmos and an elevated impression of what those hills looked like. In the centre, dwarfing everything else in the picture was a mountain, shaped like an ivory pillar. A meditating deity sheltered under a gilded temple at the summit. Circling the base were rows of rigidly symmetrical hills interspersed with trees with choreographed branches that seemed to fan the pale mountain. Animals and other gods struck poses; limbs contorted in dance; heads tilted upwards. There was a dark ocean of calligraphic waves swimming with merry-go-round horses and a ring of tiny islands. He pointed out one, "Earth". Clouds bearing gods billowed in the sky like cigar smoke and two giant lotus plants sprouted from waves bearing luminous pagodas.

"This mountain," he pointed to the ivory pillar, "is Mount Meru, the centre-of-all, where gods live and it is Kange Rinpoche in Tibet. I saw it as I left Tibet. It is a wonderful thing to see this mountain, it is seeing heaven." He traced his finger between the mountain ranges that flanked the pyramid peak to the lower half of the picture, "this is how I come, away from Kange Rinpoche through these mountains to India."

I didn't understand – was this a picture of Tibet, or of the Buddhist Heaven?

"Both."

The mountain at the centre was the heart of the Buddhist universe but it also existed on earth – and that mountain was just across the border in Western Tibet. It was a holy mountain. It was the first time I had come across the idea of a holy mountain and it immediately struck me as something that made perfect sense. Of course heaven should be a mountain – unattainable, beautiful, sometimes destructive – this was a place where gods would live. "It is east a few hundred miles from here. Pilgrims go there every year to walk round the mountain. But the borders are closed. From here we cannot go. I will not see it again."

He talked about the other mandalas, teaching me the names of the deities but when I wrote my diary in the evening I had already forgotten them. I could only remember Kange Rinpoche, the mountain we call Mount Kailash - the heavenly mountain at the centre of the world.

*

Two years passed after those university holiday travels in India. I went to work in a Bank in London, but within a few months I suspected that my career choice had been a mistake. A further year passed and I worked impossibly hard on the sale of a huge British drinks company to a huge American drinks company, and had time for little else. Every few weeks the management changed its mind on what, out of its huge stable of businesses it was going to sell, which meant that I had to change the increasingly complex financial models in all-night spreadsheet sessions, or redo a marketing document that had been perfect until they decided they wanted to keep a particular sweet, sickly, cash-generative alcopop brand. I had been a historian at university and had little training or experience in financial accounts. At eleven at night the office air conditioning was turned off and I sweated my way through screens of Microsoft Excel and dreamt about them, still sweating, when at last I slept. After multiple all night sessions I developed a sickly pallor and my body forgot to repair itself.

Things got nastier in the office as we were gripped by the economic downturn of late 2001. Colleagues were called into corner offices, blinds ominously drawn and watched by security guards as they cleared their desks. There was less business but more work as we scrabbled after clients in increasingly ruthless competition with the rest of the City (and I suppose with each other.)

I decided I would finish my two-year contract and then set off on the trip that I had always wanted to make. In my office cubicle, behind piles of printed papers, I counted off the months. When I went for morning coffee or for long breaks in the toilet cubicles (the mornings were generally the slow times), I carried a client presentation, but inside was always a guidebook or a map of the Himalayas.

I was intrigued by the idea of the holy mountain that I had first heard about in Ladakh. But I discovered that Mount Kailash was not the only one and that holy mountains were not only a Buddhist phenomenon. They featured worldwide, across countries and religions: Mount Athos, Mount Fuji, Ayers Rock, Huayna Pichu, Bear Butte, Ol Doinyo Lengai - Greece, Japan, Australia, Peru, USA, Tanzania, there are examples in every populated continent. It seemed common across many cultures to link the divine to high places. Mountains stretch closest to the heavens and their scale and drama echoes the supernatural: the placid transcendence of shining peaks, the destructive wrath of storms and rockfall. Mountains are the halfway house between earth and heaven where gods counselled and inspired men to spread their message, rules and laws were transcribed by men listening to gods on mountains, spiritual leaders meditated and received divine advice in mountain retreats, and in certain religions the gods live permanently on the summits among the spindrift and cloud.

My route took shape in these stolen planning sessions. In my mind I traced a snaking line between the holy mountains I'd visit, one in each country, one for each religion; a series of consecutive, diverse, pilgrimages that would take me from China to Turkey, walking among pilgrims, vaguely following some frayed strand of the silk road.

Maps folded, my guidebook re-concealed I'd return to my desk, my polystyrene coffee cup, my reconditioned air and the circular references of my collapsing discounted-cash-flow-analysis.

*

There had been some talk about "needing a presence in the office on Christmas day in case there are any surprises," the kind of macho remarks thrown around which made my stomach lurch, but thankfully it had come to nothing. I was glad to have made it back up to Edinburgh. I was sitting in a pub in the New Town, moaning about my life to Simon, a friend since primary school.

I told him that in six months I'd be free from investment banking and that I hoped to traverse Asia weaving between five holy mountains, taking the slow road back to Europe. I'd start at Emei Shan in China, which Buddhist pilgrims had been climbing for hundreds of years. Next would be Mount Kailash that I'd heard about four years before; a mountain revered not only by Buddhists, but by Hindus, Jainists and Bonnists. Then I'd cross the border to Mount Sulemein in Kyrgyzstan, known as Little Mecca and a site of pilgrimage for Muslims. After that I'd visit the Iranian mountain temple complex of Chak-Chak, the most important pilgrimage site for what remained of the Zoroastrian faith. Finally, there would be Mount Ararat - the highest peak in Turkey and the landing place of Noah's Ark - a biblical holy mountain: A slice of Asia, a spectrum of religions and races, ancient pilgrims and vast landscapes. It was about 5,000 miles and would take at least four months.

"Count me in." Simon's degree was due to finish at the same time and he planned to begin a career in photojournalism. This trip was the perfect opportunity to build up a portfolio with more exotic photographs than he had managed at university fashion shows. Until that point I had not imagined anything but travelling alone. Serious adventurers didn't take a mate along for company. But it seemed like a very good idea to me. Simon and I have that easygoing rapport of those who have known each other since childhood. We had been embarrassed in front of and embarrassed by each other so many times in the dramas of adolescence that we would be perfectly prepared for the close living that travel involves.

At that point, so far from the road, the anticipation of the journey was at its sweetest. We felt like heroes.

*

We left in a flurry of sleeping bags, bootlaces, and rolls of film, characteristic of the beginnings of an adventure, with a final desperate rush to Heathrow because the Iranian embassy had temporarily mislaid our passports...

At last we were airborne, moving after eight months of restless gestation.

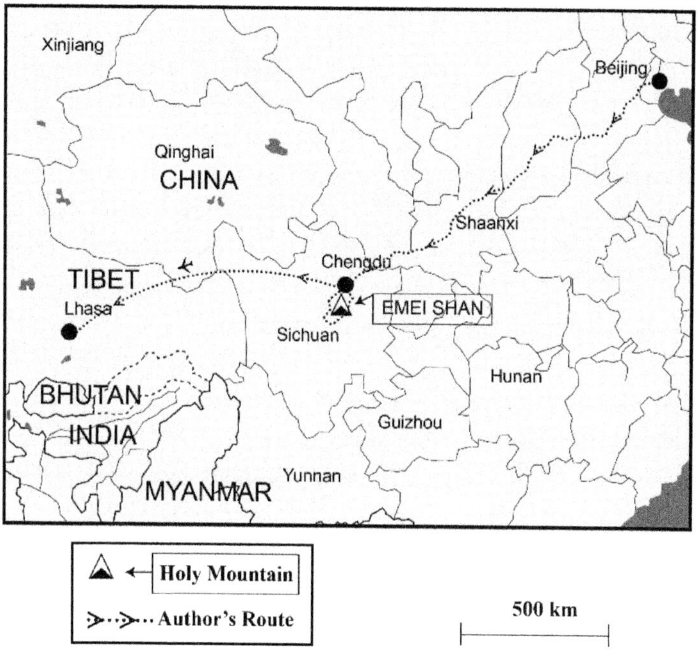
Xinjiang
Beijing
Qinghai
CHINA
Shaanxi
Chengdu
TIBET
Lhasa
EMEI SHAN
Sichuan
Hunan
BHUTAN
Guizhou
INDIA
Yunnan
MYANMAR
Holy Mountain
Author's Route
500 km

Chapter 1

Emei Shan

The train was gently swaying as scratchy waltz music was playing through the carriage speakers. I was lying beneath a seat, my legs sticking out into the aisle and my back forced into a contortion by the supports. There was a sheet of the Beijing Youth Daily below me, donated by a well-meaning fellow passenger the previous evening, when he saw me preparing to sleep on the bare floor. It was a confusing place to wake up in. I pulled myself out, stepped over Simon's legs which were sticking out into the aisle a little further down the carriage and slumped awkwardly back into my seat.

The sun was still low, casting a milky light over a new landscape. I'd fallen asleep as we rattled through the outskirts of Beijing. The landscape there had been flat with dusty roads and lines of parched fields interrupted by long, low, industrial buildings and institutional-looking farmhouses. Now the pace of the train slowed and the ground was steep and rocky. We trundled through crumbling gorges that cut between dusty brown peaks and gave the impression of traversing a giant dried river bed. Later in the day the landscape would change again from dry and brittle hills to well-watered mountains furred with trees, soft edged against the pale sky.

The carriage was now awake. The waltz was replaced by a military march with shouted instructions to accompany morning exercises. The passengers rose wearily to their feet and shuffled into place so that there was room to swing their arms. The exercises were led by the two blue-uniformed and white-gloved fuwuyuans, the female attendants who supervised our carriage. They controlled the tea point, where we were reprimanded for using the wrong cups. They ordered the bag storage; tutting at inefficiently used space and every few hours they raced the food trolley up the aisle serving up fried noodles or rice scooped from a large plastic sack. The fuwuyuans were not enthusiastic about leading the morning exercises; the carriage was not obedient like the regimented rows of department store employees we had seen in Beijing the morning before. For five minutes I swung my arms with most of the rest of the carriage (not Simon who was still asleep with his legs across the aisle). At the front, a group of teenagers made exaggeratedly expansive stretches and smirked at the younger of the exercise leaders with eyes half-taunting, half-flirting.

Our fuwuyuans looked weary from a sleepless night and now after the exercises their faces were greased with a sheen of perspiration. Their mood was not improved by a mother who had held her baby daughter over a plastic bag in the aisle to have her morning crap. The mother and baby had got on in the night at one of the isolated country stops where we would see children defecating in the street through their split crotch trousers (a sensible arrangement that avoided the need for nappies). However the fuwuyuans were insistent that Beijing standards were maintained in their carriage, and berated the mother as she was hustled along to dispose of the mess in the toilet cubicle.

All day we rolled on, stopping at stations lined with old rolling stock, where passengers got on and crowded the standing room at the end of the carriages. Our fellow Beijing to Chengdu long-haul passengers had been concerned with jockeying for sleeping space the previous evening, but now turned their attention to us with a familiarity born of a night of shared discomfort.

Tsangau was 37 and owned a drill-making factory, which he had bought in 1992 when certain regulations on private ownership were relaxed. He hated long journeys like this and was only travelling "soft seat" because the sleeper carriages had been full. He wanted to make this point clear. It was *not* because he could not afford a sleeper berth. His business demanded such travel; it was tough, but he believed Confucius was right,

"In his twenties a man's chief attention is to himself, in his thirties his chief attention must be to his family and his job. That is why you can do journeys. You men are in your twenties. I must work." Each word was considered and stressed with a flick of his thin moustache. He began to talk about China, "Mao was the law, now the PEOPLE are the law… We are growing greater with the West, together. China is a modern country. CHINA WILL INCREASE ITS GDP. The West must not forget China."

He described a powerful and unstoppable ongoing development. "Twenty years ago you would not be on this train. Fifteen years ago I would not be talking to you, ten years ago I can become a businessman, in ten or maybe twenty years time, Chinese people will be rich and travelling across Europe just like you are travelling across China". He smiled at such a symmetrical and ordered progression of history.

When he had finished he moved aside for the students, who had lined up behind him to speak to us. It was the beginning of the summer holidays and the lack of berths in the sleeper carriages was due to the mass movement of students back to university. We had chosen one of the worst weeks to take a long train journey in China.

Outside, the whole day passed with the steady clatter of rails, darkness eventually falling on an endless progression of patchwork fields and cracked ridges.

*

Although there are many Buddhist holy mountains locally revered across China, there are four mountains of national renown that have been attracting pilgrims for centuries: Wu Tai Shan, Jiu Hua Shan, Pu Tuo Shan and Emei Shan. They lie at the four points of the compass, each one linked to a particular deity.

Holy mountains are crucial in the Buddhist spiritual tradition as places where devotees can pay homage to their deities and where they can free themselves from the material trappings and luxuries of everyday life. Most importantly pilgrims can witness Buddha in the natural surroundings. Sometimes Buddha is physically represented: the island of Pu Tuo Shan is said to look like a reclining Buddha, while the Emei Shan massif resembles the elephant which the Bodhisattva Pu Sa rides on. More abstractly, pilgrims can make out the image of Buddha in all the natural beauty of the mountain: the waterfalls, pools, cloud formations and vistas, an idea summed up in the saying, "Buddha is mountain, mountain is Buddha."

We were to climb Emei Shan, the westerly holy mountain lying near Chengdu in Sichuan province. The name means Lofty Eyebrow Mountain, a reference to the shape of the tree covered summit, which looks like the curve of an eyebrow when clouds obscure the lower slopes. An alternative explanation for the name is that the character has altered and that it should really mean "young daughter" in memory of a local farmer whose daughters became the mountains. The combination of odd stories and not-quite-remembered name roots felt familiar to me with my experience of Scottish mountains. These wild, untamed landscapes create room for myths and fantasies, for anthropomorphism and for the belief that they hold some not-yet-understood power.

Emei Shan is dedicated to Pu Sa, the Bodhisattva of Perfection and patron of the Lotus Sutra, the book which discusses how those in difficulties on earth can be rescued by compassionate Bodhisattvas. These are merciful beings who have reached the level of perfection to slip into Nirvana but who choose to use their merit to help save those who are still suffering on earth.

Buddhism is sometimes seen as a rather solitary faith requiring a single-handed, personal struggle to reach Nirvana. However the presence of Bodhisattvas balances this view, stressing generosity of spirit and the importance of helping one's community - perfection for the individual is not possible without perfection for all. Pu Sa is a vital symbol of this selfless philosophy and is revered across Buddhist China.

*

We were standing in the queue for the Emei Shan ticket office behind a petite Chinese girl in white halter-neck top and white denim pedal-pushers. She was shouting hurriedly down her mobile phone. The pace sped up until, exasperated, she snapped it shut and let it drop so that it hung against her chest, a tiny silver Motorola on a luminous cord. She smiled amusedly at our full rucksacks; all she was carrying was a silver handbag.

"I was talking to my boyfriend in Beijing," she started in confident English. "Well *maybe* he is my boyfriend. Are you climbing up?"

"Yes."

"I am going up too, in the lift." She pointed towards the cable car station. "I am with the Canadians," a middle-aged couple stood some distance away. "You should come in the lift too. It is too many steps I think." She watched us with upraised eyebrows that made me think she enjoyed making boys feel awkward.

I mumbled with mock stoicism. "No, we'll climb the whole thing."

"Why?"

It was early in the trip, and the plan of our adventure was still fresh in my mind. I told her about all the holy mountains in countries stretching all the way across Asia to Turkey.

"Why?" She asked with a little smile.

"Well, why are *you* going up? Are you a pilgrim?"

"No, I am a tour guide."

"Are you a religious tour guide?"

"No, I am not religious. No one is religious. My friends - not religious. My family - not religious. I think it is a stupid thing – it just stops you from eating some things."

The car park at the base of Emei Shan was busy but it was not what I had expected. I had imagined it to be serene and exotic. To satisfy his photographic ambitions I had promised Simon wrinkled faces of pilgrims in bare landscapes. I had promised him pages of The National Geographic. But most of the visitors were students enjoying their university holidays. Lines of coaches disgorged crowds, which seethed around the ticket office, minute cameras hanging from their wrists. The girls were dressed uniformly in skin-tight three-quarter length trousers, strappy shoes and designer tops bearing logos in big letters. They looked dressed more for Saturday night clubbing than a mountain climb.

We'd had that awkward, out-of-place feeling since we'd arrived in the crowds of Beijing: the sense that our limbs were too long and unwieldy and our features over-sized and clumsy looking. In the crowds of black-haired heads we felt conspicuous. Simon has sandy brown hair and my hair, although dark, does not lie flat. Both of us are over six foot. To make matters worse we had decided to grow beards, for convenience and slightly childishly perhaps to signify our embrace of a new nomadic life. But in these bristly early stages they didn't look good. Simon's growth was scattered, sparse and wispy across his face while mine left my jaw bare. We looked an unconvincing pair. We wore hiking boots and "breathable" fabrics, and carried bulky rucksacks that pulled at our shoulders and forced us to lean forward awkwardly. We were still in that state of over-equipped cluelessness that characterises the newly arrived traveller – just setting out.

"See you later," sang the tour guide as she collected her tickets and gave a last sympathetic look at our packs, or was it our outfits? At the ticket office our photographs were instantly laser-printed onto the tickets with a stack of digital technology so we could not sell our passes on to anyone else. It was an early indication that this holy mountain had been hauled into modernity.

A cable car climbs the first few hundred metres to one of the most extensive sites on the mountain, Wangnian Temple. It took us an hour to walk the same distance. The path became gradually steeper and we were soon sweating heavily. Little streams ran between the trees humidifying the air and watering the vegetation, which hung like a heavy blanket all around us. Perspiration ran down from my scalp into my eyes and seeped from my back to soak my rucksack straps. Stripped to the waist, we plodded on, already regretting the weight of our packs.

The crowds from the car park reappeared at the top of the cable car, and the front of the Wangnian Temple was a chaotic scene of posers and photographers vying for space. The tour guide appeared from the temple, busily texting on her mobile, her tired-looking Canadians a few metres behind her. She saw us recovering from the shock of the first hour of climbing and pulled out her camera, thrusting it into one of the Canadian's hands.

"Can I have my picture with you?" She put her arms around our shoulders, then quickly lifted them, realising we were soaked with sweat. "You have passed the Cave of the White Dragon," she launched into her guide-monologue. "It is called this because once there was a bad snake but it was a beautiful white snake. One day it turned itself into a beautiful girl and married a man. He was very happy with her and did not realise she was a snake. One day he came to the mountain and the monk told him the snake was bad and he locked her into the cave so she could not escape." Each word was hyphenated to the next – rattled off at high speed. But the story felt similar to folk tales we knew, simple mountain tales that tried to make sense of landscapes that moved us or made us fearful.

"Now," she turned to the bemused Canadians, her express-guiding over. "We go down in the lift, back to the bus, and then we will drive to the summit. OK? Then lunch." They straggled off after her obediently. " Goodbye boys."

*

In the first dome-roofed hall of Wangnian temple sat Pu Sa in the middle of a lotus flower that was perched on top of his gold-tusked, white elephant. This was a tenth century painted bronze statue almost ten metres high built to celebrate his visit to the mountain in the sixth century. All around the side of the room were perched shelf upon shelf of foot high metal Buddhas, three hundred and seven in all, representing the benefactors who gave money for the temple to be built. In the courtyard pools, ornamental carp sent ripples across the still surfaces as they gulped floating flies. Beside the pools were flaming torches. These all had a purpose according to the Buddhist view of the world: the smoke from the torches linked the temples to the spirit world, the carp pools repelled evil spirits and were arranged in such a way as to prevent the spirits from entering (evil spirits are held to be hydrophobic and can only travel in straight lines).

But despite the Buddhist-focussed planning of the Wangnian Temple, now it seemed principally set up to accommodate sightseers. While Simon was photographing the statue of Pu Sa astride his elephant a monk beckoned to him. I thought this was a signal to stop his intrusive photography, but he turned out to be showing Simon a better position to take the photograph from. Inside the gateway of the temple a large "BUDDHIST SHOP" sold figurines, books and tapes and played Chinese Classical music on a loop. This was the most popular area of the temple and bands of visitors chattered excitedly over souvenir soft toys and soapstone Buddha-shaped incense holders (a hole drilled into his bald smiling head to hold the stick.)

I'd been reading the account of an earlier traveller to this region. André Migot spent years in China during the turbulent 1940s when civil war and banditry were destroying the country. He was a Buddhist convert, fascinated by the spiritual life of the country and when he climbed Emei Shan in 1946 he described the pilgrims with great admiration.

"I was greatly struck by the seriousness with which they took the whole business. Nothing gives the Chinese greater pleasure than conversation or, failing that, meditation; but these pilgrims hardly ever halted, never dawdled, and scarcely exchanged a word. They pressed on steadily in single file, wasting no time…They did not miss out a single shrine or a single temple, and they paid their respects to every image with the same dutiful formula, lighting one stick of incense and prostrating themselves once."[1]

Yet how different were these chattering, clicking visitors who arrived by cable car now and thronged around the Buddhist shop. Migot would not have recognised them at all.

Migot himself was a serious pilgrim too. He had ambitious plans to travel widely in China and smuggle himself all the way to the holy city of Lhasa. But the difficulties of travel in war-torn China of the 1940s meant that the unfortunate Frenchman kept running into trouble. Having climbed Emei Shan, he was attacked by bandits and lost all of his equipment and money and had to scale back his plans. He was arrested on the road to Lhasa, before he even got to Tibet, and just as he thought his troubles were over he was kidnapped by the Red Army and held captive for two weeks in the hills of

---

[1] "Tibetan Marches," Andre Migot. English Translation by Peter Fleming. Penguin 1957.

Manchuria. In his introduction to the English translation Peter Fleming writes with typical understatement that "Dr Migot has had – and I suspect, will continue to have – a varied life."

*

Above the cable car and Wangnian temple the steps were less busy, although there was always a group within a couple of hundred metres of us. Most of the other climbers were students, laughing their way up, uttering horrified cries and fits of giggles whenever the next stretch of steps was revealed.

It is strange to climb a 3,000m peak on stairs - the whole way. The level of work that had gone into putting steps all the way up the mountain was impressive but walking on them for hours on end was monotonous and eventually painful.

We both developed blisters on our untrained feet. When we stopped to rest at a tea-house we took off socks and shoes and soothed our feet under the outdoor tap.

To avoid the pain of climbing these tiring steps it's possible to be carried up the mountain in a litter. Green-waistcoated carriers with silver badges on their sleeves take each end of the litter and climb the steps at a regular, exhausting trot. I couldn't help laughing when we saw the first party making an ascent like this. In front, was a large portly gentleman with dark glasses and cigarette in hand, and his carriers gasping beneath him. Behind him was his tiny wife, clearly the easier load; and the mother in law in the rear, looking slightly embarrassed by how much her bearers were perspiring.

The litter carriers were not the only beasts of burden on the mountain. Coolies carried stones to repair the steps and food supplies to the restaurants and monasteries on the route up the mountain. They used wooden frames with shoulder straps to carry huge sacks of rice, which projected high above their heads. In their hands they had stout wooden sticks which they banged on each step and stuck under the frame to take the weight from their shoulders when they rested. We could hear them by the firm "clack" of their sticks well before we saw them, trudging painfully in long slow lines. Some carried fresh vegetables and slabs of meat on a two-dished yoke which they hung from one shoulder. These looked the most awkward loads of all, their single shoulder red and inflamed, their bodies weeping sweat. On their feet they wore rope-soled sandals or army-issue olive plimsolls. They were all young and mostly emaciated but with bulging calf muscles.

As we ascended, the temples became smaller and quieter. In Chudian palace there was only a solitary Buddha of modest proportions. In front of this a woman slept, slumped over her knitting. At Xixiang Chi, the Elephant Bathing pool where Pu Sa is said to have washed his white elephant, the hermitage was silent and the three figures on the dais looked out over an empty hall.

The gradient of the path eased as it ran along a narrow ridge bitten with crenellations that revealed steep gullies sweeping down into a swirling void of cloud. Within the cloud we came across the monkeys who live all over Emei Shan in a semi-domestic relationship with the tourists and monks. They sat on the temple's walls, searching one another for fleas and nervously approached us to touch our shoes and hold out their hands for food. They were attractive animals; their eyes close together above a light pink nose, their faces fringed with stiff grey hair. The official tourist map for the mountain tells visitors that although "the monkeys are not dangerous it is better to appease them." We did so, with biscuits.

*

It was slightly disheartening to have climbed for seven hours on thousands of steps to reach a busy coach stop. The road ascends the mountain from the other side and only meets the path at this point, before the last ridge. For a few hundred metres on either side of the bus park the paths were busy again, medicine booths with counters heaped with strange looking funguses lined the car park.

"Mister, Mister, medicine here, very good for tiredness…"
There was a choice of mono-rail or cable car (or more steps) from the car park to the summit, which meant the footpath quietened down again as we kept on climbing above the road-head. It was two more hours to the summit, during which time the sun fell in the sky and a damp coldness crept in from the forest.

At last we pulled our way up the last few steps to the Jinding Peak, (Golden Peak) and looked around us. It was like being on the edge of the world. In front of us to the east the mountain dropped away in hundreds of metres of vertical cliffs to meet a sea of clouds stretching flat to the horizon. To the West piles of clouds spiralled upwards into the sky as if they were trying to suffocate the dying sun. We were standing on the rock-strewn plateau between two majestic buildings: the Woyan Nunnery, a large elegant barn-like building made of wood painted a deep maroon and the Jinding Temple, a multi-layered building with upturned roof piled upon upturned roof. The roof was, at one time, made from bronze, which is how the Golden Peak got its name, but now it is covered with glazed tiles. A bell hung from the temple, and a monk was striking it slowly with a curved stick, sending out a sad chime, a sign to the gods that they were ready to pray. Apart from this the plateau was empty, windless, and quiet.

"Our first holy mountain. Four more to go." We grinned at each other with tired eyes and shook hands casually because too much congratulation seemed wrong at what was really the beginning of our journey. We stood there for a few minutes, not speaking, caught up in our own thoughts. The journey seemed real now, we were really going to give it a shot – but it had been an exhausting day and there were a lot of miles to go until Turkey.

A shadow fell across us; the sun was extinguished by the mounting clouds. Somewhere far away, behind the spiralling mist, cold blue lightning flickered and several seconds later came the muffled sound of thunder. I shivered, cold now that I had stopped moving and put my shirt back on.

*

The promotional material on Mount Emei lists its "Four Famous View:" These are, "the cloud sea, the saint lamp, the Buddhist light, and the sunrise." The first view we had seen the previous night. The second is a phenomenon caused by swarms of fireflies streaming upwards in formation, which early pilgrims decided must be a form of homage paid by the insect world to the Lord Buddha. This is unfortunately rarely to be seen except on the warmest of summer nights. The Buddhist light or "Buddha's glory" is the name given to what we call the Brocken spectre, where the viewer's shadow is projected by the sun onto a bank of clouds. While a group may all see the spectre, each person will only be able to see their own solitary shadow often surrounded by a luminous rainbow. Our forerunner, Migot related that sometimes pilgrims were so overcome by the sight of the brocken spectre that they threw themselves off the cliff towards it. However, like Migot we were not to be blessed with the precise conditions of sun and cloud required for the vision so we decided we should get up early and see the fourth "famous view", the sunrise.

It was dark when we pulled our aching limbs out of bed but the guesthouse was already awake and it looked like the sunrise was going to be popular. Crowds were gathering on the summit, hundreds of small figures, huddled together in identical brightly coloured padded overcoats, which were available to hire for one yuan at the coach park. We stumbled along the terrace with stiff knees and joined the string of tourists lining the terrace, cold fingers fiddling with dials on their cameras.

Half an hour later the first glimmer appeared - a pink ellipse, submerged but slowly rising to the surface. A faint cheer went up and a louder one when the full circle appeared from the sea of clouds, flooding the monastery with orange and pink light. Flashes went off all around the viewing terrace as if a winning goal had been scored. The thunder of the previous night had not cleared the clouds from the sky, and the sun hung only briefly, like a perfectly circular, glowing coal, caught between horizon and cloud line, before vanishing upwards. The event over, the crowds dispersed to the instant-noodle stalls while the light flattened to a neutral grey.

Monks and nuns, all with close-cropped hair, walked purposefully across the plateau and took up their positions by the huge brass bells on the temple. Two prostrated themselves before the dimly lit Buddha in the Woyan nunnery while a group of visitors surrounded them and let off strobe-like flashes from their cameras. I cringed at their intrusiveness as they hovered round the altars; pointing their cameras at the monks' faces and making them blink. The monks carried on praying like actors in a play. Further down the west side of the mountain I could see the gaunt car parks and skeletal lifts of the Emei Shan ski resort, another sign of the mountain's shift from pilgrimage to tourist destination.

I had imagined these holy mountains to be a keyhole onto an unblemished country; free from the increasingly enveloping soup of commercial culture. But in among the crowds I felt that hypocritical disappointment of the adventurous tourist when he finds himself among so many other tourists. I resented them for taking the easy way up and defiling the mountain with a cable car and a road and I resented them because I saw a reflection of my camera-wielding-self in them. None of us was a real pilgrim.

But it was easy to escape them. We just took to the footpaths and went the long way down on the eastern ridge making a full circuit of the system of steps. The eastern path was a longer route, but wilder and more spectacular; it clung to the side of the cliff overhung by rock and precarious looking trees. Beneath the path thundered the river, waterfall after crashing waterfall. We could hear it constantly but only glimpsed the white of rushing water through the curtain of branches. It felt good to get away from the shops and crowds. We contoured the steep river gully and I felt as though I was walking through an ancient Chinese print. Above me the white line of a steep river, flanked by thickets of green bamboo led up to a small pagoda perched on a tree-fringed limestone spur.

A fine mist hung in the air giving the scene a soft, watercolour focus.

There were few parties making their way up these paths and for long periods it was only the two of us, walking in single file along stone paths through the jungle. The tea shops which had been every hundred metres on the way up were less frequent now, and we always took the excuse to stop and buy large bottles of Wangxu water, *official mineral water of the Beijing 2008 Olympics*.

The temples were quieter on this path and even less elaborate than some of the tea-houses on the western path. In one of them we came across a group that looked different from the other visitors. Three of them seemed as old as the mountain, backs bent, faces furrowed and coloured a deep oily brown. They wore long Tibetan coats (chubas) tied at the waist, grimy and ragged. They looked at us with curious smiles as we entered the room where they were resting. They had laid down their belongings at one side of the altar - three small cloth-wrapped packages bound with twine and three prayer wheels, motionless now, after a day of spinning. Prayer wheels look like rattles, a small barrel at the end of a stick containing a scrap of paper with the letters of a prayer written in Sanskrit. While walking, the pilgrims turn the barrel with a flick of the wrist committing a constant round of prayers to the gods.

Their guide was younger and wore the uniform of monks; baggy trousers that tightened around the calves and a plain smock with a neat round collar, all made of the same grey flannel material. He was Chinese and lived in Emei Shan village where he helped with the organisation of the monasteries. He was helping three elderly pilgrims who had arrived the week before in the village, almost penniless. "They are from Yunnan province," he told us, "from near Zhong

Dien," an area politically part of Yunnan but geographically part of the Tibetan plateau and populated by ethnic Tibetans. "This mountain is very holy to them. Very important to them, and they make a pledge to come here before they die. They are Tibetans you see. Emei Shan is the mountain of Pu Sa, the thinking Buddha. Tibetans call him Chenrézik. So they are coming to the mountain of Chenrézik." The pilgrims smiled and nodded at us in recognition of the name. Their map-like faces, eyes creased to pupil's width, spoke of their home on that vast high land. I felt a surge of excitement that we would soon be going there.

The guide's name was Lu Guang Yi and he chided us for rushing the mountain. "We come here to think too, like Pu Sa, not just to walk. Important to do it slowly. Walk slowly like the elephant of Pu Sa. To see mountain see temples. No hurry. No hurry." He smiled at us and I felt guilty that we were in such a rush. The pilgrims would sleep here tonight in the corner of the temple and continue on their slow way tomorrow, while we were descending all the way to the bottom and would be in Chengdu by evening.

I asked Lu Guang Yi if this really still was a holy mountain, and he nodded. He knew that the visitors with prayer wheels were vastly outnumbered by the visitors with cameras.

"Many visitors are not praying, just looking at the temple, looking at the monkeys. But there are some that want to think about Buddhism and come to talk to the monks... some. But China is not a religious country anymore. It has been too difficult." he shrugged. Lu Guang Yi sat silently for some time, pondering what he had said or what he would say. "The older people have been broken from these traditions so the young people do not know them. There are few pilgrims now and there are fewer monks than there have been. But monks are still here ready for the pilgrims, and this mountain will always be holy with us."

A monk brought in a tray of tea in small grey bowls that matched his tunic. It was jasmine tea, delicate and almost colourless, with all the flavour in the aroma rather than the taste. At the bottom of the bowl the loose leaves unrolled in the hot water and released tiny white flowers that floated to the top.

Lu Guang Yi carried on talking quietly, the monk who had brought us the tea lit incense in front of the statue and one of the Tibetans fell asleep. This little temple was a haven, inaccessible by vehicle and primitive so that even if tourists might look in, they did not stay for long. In the peace of the forest the monks were uninterrupted as they performed their daily rituals and ministered to the visiting pilgrims. I wanted to stay longer but we had not been generous enough with our time on the mountain.

*

The forest got denser as we descended and the air was thick and heavy. Insects swarmed around my sweating face and each step jarred my knees. Coming down felt even more difficult than going up. Whenever we stopped we seized up, and the next flight of steps became even more painful. Simon was complaining about an old football injury aggravated by the repetitive strain of the descent. "I should have had surgery you know. There's still a bit of loose cartilage in my knee joint. I'll never play again… are you listening?"

We came upon a pool in the river in which a group of boys were playing, jumping, hollering from the rocks at the side. We jumped in too and surfaced, winded by the freezing mountain water. The boys swam, otter like underwater and caught tiny red fish in their hands. One emerged with the back half of a fish clamped between his teeth. Its back half wriggled where it emerged from his mouth and he spat it out onto the rocks, laughing.

After seven hours of descent the crowds that we had left on the summit appeared again, and we knew it could not be far to the road. The paths got wider and a large sign announced that we had entered the "Joking Monkey Zone," a series of raised pathways and rope bridges where visitors could feed the monkeys. The monkeys posed, arms outstretched for nuts while the crowds fired volleys of camera shots. The pagodas here were gaudy and housed rubbish bins rather than deities. The concrete handrails had been painted and sculpted to look like gnarled wood but ended up looking tatty. The noises of the forest were replaced with the cacophony of human noises: shouts, sales-talk "Mister Mister..." and engines revving in the nearby car park. Groups of litter carriers lay slumped by a tea stand underneath a multi-lingual sign, which promised that these employees of the Emei Shan management would not subject the customer to "rudeness, bad words or unfair prices." The paths were once again crowded with souvenir shops selling fake jade bracelets, medicinal tea and cuddly monkeys. We were back in the Emei Shan theme park.

The road head was a bustling chaos. Cars competed with shuttle-buses to edge into the queue leaving the car park. We piled onto the bus headed for Emei Shan village where we had begun the day before, and connected with a coach for Chengdu. We were part of the crowd of tourists again, catered for with ruthless efficiency: regular buses, litter patrols, coats for hire, souvenir booths, three different ways up the mountain (none of which involved physical effort) and the opportunity to photograph with impunity. Fifty years of communism and now an all-consuming desire to industrialise and modernise had severed this mountain from its pilgrims.

I was glad we had met Lu Guang Yi and had been told to walk more like an elephant. It was comforting to think that when the wheels on the cable car had stopped turning, when the shops had been shuttered up and the car parks had emptied, Lu Guang Yi and his Yunnan pilgrims would be asleep on the mountain in the single-roomed temple. The next day their prayer wheels would begin spinning again to Chenrézik, to Pu Sa, on the most important pilgrimage of their life.

CHAPTER 2

Lhasa

Splashes of water spun from the wheels as the plane touched down on Lhasa airstrip. A thin mist draped itself over low, brown mountains and the runway gave off the metallic smell of fresh rain on tarmac. The two-hour drive from the airport to Lhasa was across wide stretches of flat tundra, which ended on the horizon in the furrows of distant mountains. This was the harsh and limitless scenery that we would become used to over the next month. Crouching figures wrapped in layers of clothing moved slowly in the fields and the dainty stacks of rice straw that we had seen in the Chinese countryside were replaced with broad stacks of barley straw. Strings of prayer flags fluttered from low monasteries that seemed to grow organically out of the hillside, their thick-ledged, square windows sturdy and protective.

Six weeks earlier, I had been sitting at my desk modelling the cash flow of leveraged-buy-out opportunities, now I was in the People's Republic of the Autonomous Region of Tibet, the land that every guidebook labelled within the first paragraph, "the roof of the world." I inhaled to confirm what I had left – no longer the smell of warm computers, paper dust and other people's coffee. Now it was diesel, plastic-leather seats, damp earth, cigarette smoke on cold air – the aromatic components not individually exotic, but somehow thrilling as a cocktail.

Tibet under Chinese rule has been a closed-off place and this political isolation has been matched by a geographical isolation; flanked by the Himalayas to one side and the wastes of the Taklamakan and Gobi deserts on the other. Tourists had little access to travel in Tibet after the Chinese took control in 1959 until 1984 when it was partially opened. This privilege was swiftly withdrawn after the violent pro-independence riots in 1987, which was embarrassingly witnessed and filmed by visitors in Lhasa. In 1992 the country was opened again with the condition that travellers must be part of a tour group, a rule which is officially still in force.

Even with these limitations the Himalayan state manages to lure tourists in substantial numbers. There were three travel agents selling tickets to Tibet, all based in small offices in the lobby of our hotel in Chengdu "Tibet Budget Tours", "Tibet Tours" and "Budget Flights". A lonely Buddha stared out from behind the glass window, through the notices advertising tour services - "Potala Experience," "Deluxe Himalayan Tour." On the walls were the classic images of Tibetan landmarks, the Potala Palace, Mount Everest, a grinning monk.

With the tourists have come Han Chinese economic migrants, the ethnic majority group in China, keen to exploit a new market. We passed a whole island of reclaimed land in the Lhasa River, packed with new workshop-houses, some not yet roofed but already occupied by industrious Chinese immigrants. The main street was cluttered with bright advertising signs and a pedestrianised shopping precinct was under construction with multi-level tile-clad shops fronted by huge plate-glass windows. In the windows posed Chinese mannequins in Western clothes, looking out with a haughty gaze at the still unfinished pavement.

In the main square photographers had set up tourist stands complete with costumes and props. I had my portrait taken as a Chinese emperor sitting on a throne, then as a Mongol warlord in the saddle of an imitation horse. Simon rolled his eyes.

Although we resented being forced to pay extra for a "budget Lhasa tour" to get around the restriction that tourists must be in a four-person tour party, it was actually quite pleasant to be led round the sites while still feeling sluggish with altitude. In the centre of Lhasa, triumphant in scale and design, stood the Potala looking proudly out over a bland municipal square. Huge sloping rectangles of red and white, punctuated by wide lines of black windows, interlocked with one another, like a giant cubist painting. The building is made up of two parts, the white palace containing the government and administrative rooms, and the red palace, made up of the chapels and shrine rooms; a combination which echoed the theocratic rule of the Dalai Lama – religious leader and head of state – embodied in one man. The thrones of past Dalai Llamas sat empty in tapestried rooms and lower down where the palace met the rock there were ranks of weighty metal stupas highlighted with jade, pearls, garnet, turquoise and lapis containing the remains of the most respected high lamas or regents.

Numerous statues crowded the altars. In the centre where the three incarnations of Buddha past, present and future flanked by numerous other deities; the medicine Buddha holding medicine bowl and herbs; and the dramatic protector deities with rolling white eyes and wide mouths, grimacing and revealing rows of fangs. In one room the walls were lined with books of Buddhist philosophy bound at the narrow edge like parchment chequebooks and in another the walls were alive with black and gold tantric murals. And yet, one couldn't help remembering that this place would be abuzz with clerks and officials, were Tibet still self-governing. Instead, the Dalai Lama and his court sit in exile in India and the empty Potala Palace is managed by the Chinese Tourist Authority. The silence was unnatural like the hush of a closed-down factory. Video cameras and motion sensors were bolted to the walls in every room, their blinking LEDs at odds with the smoke-patterned walls and carved beams. The tour ended in a carpet factory where Tibetan women tied knots all day on gaudy designs, depicting snarling snow leopards and windswept maidens. It was hard not to feel offended by the well-meaning Chinese sales men who buzzed around us.

*

The Jokaing is a series of shrines and temples connected to a monastery in the middle of Lhasa. At seven in the evening this city-centre temple was packed with locals, mumbling prayers, making circumambulations of particular shrines and emptying packets of butter into the rows of smoking lamps. Moving independently was impossible; I could only sway along with the crowd in a constant clockwise rotation that passed the door every five minutes or so. This was a working site and felt alive in a way the abandoned Potala did not; there was a rich, slightly sickly smell of unwashed clothes, incense, and burning fat from the hundreds of yak butter lamps. The light was dim and focussed on images of deities, which loomed out from alcoves and paintings on the wall. A constant murmur came from the crowds of Tibetans, prayers muttered in never-ending rounds. The main hall was filled with lines of monks who huddled in their red robes and let out a throaty humming, in one continuous hypnotic drone.

On the roof of the Jokaing, with the relief of fresh air, I watched the lowering sun set the gilt statues and bells alight. In one direction, the iceberg shape of the Potala was hazy behind an evening mist and in the other, beyond the rooftops of Lhasa, shadows leapt up the gullies of the dry mountains. Looking down from the roof, I could see the regular movements of devotees prostrating themselves repeatedly, the sound a confusion of swishing and scraping as they slid across the paving on a cardboard mat and lay down in front of the temple. They were mostly old and mostly women. They stood, hands held together in front of their chests, eyes closed before bending and kneeling, sliding their cardboard mats with their hands fully outstretched, pressing their foreheads on the paving stone. They lay for a second then pushed themselves up, raising clasped hands to foreheads and started again. Some seemed to be doing it for hours, muttering under their breath, prayers and mantras "Om me padme Om," - "Hail to the Jewel in the Lotus flower," the fundamental Buddhist mantra.

All day Simon had been like an excited child. Around every corner was a new scene, a market, an outdoor game of pool, monks chanting for alms – too many images to photograph at once. He would wander off mid-conversation with his camera glued to his face, strike up nonsense conversations with beggars and stall-holders to get their faces in the light. He missed lunch while he waited for a butcher to begin work on a yak haunch in the Muslim quarter of the city. Now at dusk on the roof of the Jokaing he called me over to play nurse to his surgeon as he swapped lenses, "Hold – lens cap – wrong one – no don't put it down – lens cleaner – hold – quickly or I'll lose the evening light." Across the Lhasa rooftops the Potala Palace was ghost-like in the evening mist and the gilded Jokaing statues glowed orange.

*

I was enjoying Lhasa, but as we acclimatised and got to know the town I couldn't help feeling restless. Mount Kailash, our next holy mountain, lay a further two thousand kilometres to the west. To get the permits required for this journey we needed to go with an official travel agency, and pay for a jeep, driver and guide. It was an expensive proposition and we could not afford it unless we found two other passengers to share the cost with.

As each day passed I became more restless. I charged across town to different travel operators asking whether anybody had recently expressed an interest in making the journey. I put up signs in all the tourist hotels advertising two free places. If we left it too long we could risk overstaying our Chinese visa.

A week later we had found our two companions for the trip west. Sandra was in her late thirties and a fully qualified homeopathic physician. She had acquired her entire travelling wardrobe in Kathmandu, tie-dyed tunics with sanskrit and wheel-of-life prints, floaty pyjama trousers, expedition surplus climbing boots, and a collection of fleeces in primary colours. She was now a Buddhist but had dabbled in various New Age philosophies and had just returned from a summer spent working in a dolphin habitat, "where humans and dolphins can live together." She spoke with a lazy drawl and an unshakeable belief in the truth of all her opinions. But she wanted to go to

Kailash too and we were not in a position to be fussy about our companions.

We were to get on much better with Julia, a half Chinese American in her forties, who had held a high powered position in Asian real estate before quitting and heading off on the Trans-Siberian railway with a thick book on Buddhism. She shared our enthusiasm for a plan I had been thinking about since we started: to somehow persuade our guide to continue west after we had been to Kailash and detach ourselves from our tour when we were in Ali, the furthest west of the Tibetan towns, then hitchhike along a high altitude road out of Tibet to Kashgar in western China. Although this would take several days it would save us a good deal of time, as it meant that we did not have to double back to Lhasa then go north of Tibet through China to reach Kashgar. However, the road to Kashgar runs across an area of disputed territory between India and China, climbs to over 5,000m, borders on the unstable Kashmir region and as a result is strictly closed to all foreigners. A few Westerners had been rumoured to get through in previous years, hiding in trucks or cycling around checkpoints, but, since the troubles had started in Afghanistan, security had been increased and it was now very difficult to go either way on the road. In some ways this just made it more attractive, a road which saved us time but was also forbidden - I told the travel agent to add Ali to our permit request.

"There is nothing to see in Ali, why you need that?" she demanded.

"We hear there are good showers there, and it is my friend's birthday, so we want a proper restaurant. It is the biggest town in the area." I answered in part truths; Simon's birthday was in three weeks time.

She put Ali on the permit with a shrug.

We handed over a hefty deposit and were told it would take a week to get all the permits necessary for our trip. Another static week was frustrating but it felt good to have the certainty of a departure date.

*

We did acclimatisation hikes on the hills around Lhasa, sunbathed on deck chairs in the hotel courtyard and ate expensive yak steaks, with the excuse that they would be full of iron and would help us to develop red blood cells. We would need all the help we could get. Lhasa sits at around 4,000m and we knew it would be a strain to make it up to the 5,700m on the circuit around Kailash. We bought supplies: jerry cans for water, dust masks, noodles, biscuits, sun hats (cowboy style, an essential for the well dressed Tibetan man), army surplus long johns and army surplus jackets (the jackets for warmth as well as disguise should we need it during our illegal hitch-hike west). They were olive green with a dark brown fake-fur collar that folded up to well above the ears, and thickly padded with a canvas-like material that made the whole thing extremely heavy. It felt as if it might be bullet proof.

One afternoon I left Simon photographing in the market and cycled to the outskirts of Lhasa leaving my hired bike where the track became too steep and rough. My lungs burned as I continued my climb on foot, and there was a ferric taste of dry air and exertion in my mouth. Panting, I crossed dry riverbeds, the sides loose with dust and scree. Then it was back onto the opposite bank where wiry scrub kept the desiccated earth together in clumps. On the other side of the hill, another path twisted upwards, a series of tight hairpin bends picked out in yellow grit. At the top I could see the cluster of buildings in white and red, the monastic colours of the Pabonka temple that I was heading for.

I was sweating and panting when I reached it. A monk with a limp and a gravelly voice came out with a huge key for the temple door. This is the oldest religious building in the Lhasa area, set on a granite boulder dropped by a retreating glacier thousands of years before. Inside, it was dark after the brightness of the afternoon. A rectangle of cushions sat in the centre surrounded by a grey-red balustrade. The walls were lined with glass cabinets, imprisoning statues whose faces and poses were becoming gradually familiar to me. The monk who had let me in gestured for me to help him by carrying round a metal bucket into which he emptied the seven dishes of water that had stood before the various shrines around the room. (Standing in front of the statues for twenty-four hours had blessed the water and it could now be used in holy functions.)

When he had finished he tugged on my elbow and in a low voice asked, "Dalai Llama?"

The Chinese have decreed that possession of pictures of the current Dalai Llama are illegal and destroy all images of him found in monasteries and houses. Images of the spiritual and political leader in exile remain highly valued by Tibetans and frequently we would be asked if we had his picture. I opened my guidebook where there was a simple black and white drawing of the current Dalai Llama and passed it to the old monk. He stared at it in silence and lifted the book to press the open page against his forehead, muttering something under his breath. He thanked me with sad eyes as he passed it back.

It was quiet on the top of the temple. I could see across to the expanse of Lhasa and beyond to the river, and the hills on the other side of the valley. It was a big city now. The jumble of houses in the centre - the old town - contrasted with the wide sweeping thoroughfares, which led out to regimented concrete developments and the river islands covered with new buildings. Beyond the urban sprawl the ground was covered with acres of polythene tunnels where a fertile atmosphere was created from the harsh Tibetan terrain for cultivation. From this point it was easy to see what the old Lhasa must have been like, a disorganised warren of mud brick houses around the sacred Potala set in the middle of a vast flood plain. The Summer Palace to the West would have been a country retreat, not encircled as it was now with new developments.

*

The first European to reach Tibet was Friar Orderic of Pordenone in 1328.

"I came to a certain great kingdom called Tibet, which is on the confines of India Proper, and is subject to the Great Khan… The folk of that country dwell in tents made of black felt. But the chief and royal city is all built with walls of black and white, and all its streets are very well paved. In this city no one shall dare to shed blood of any, whether man or beast, for the reverence they bear a certain idol which is there worshipped."[2]

I first came across Orderic while studying for a paper on the history of the Franciscan Order at university. He was a Franciscan, an explorer and an early practitioner of that strange amalgam of fact and fiction that is most travel writing. He entered the Order at Udine in the early 1300s, a time when the

---

[2] "The Travels of Friar Orderic." Orderic of Pordenone, translated by Henry Yule, Hakluyt Society 1916.

Franciscans were experiencing the turmoil inherent in the expansion of any organisation. St Francis had died in 1226 and the order had split into opposing factions. One side wanted the friars to remain true to the original rule of absolute poverty while the other saw entry into the world of academia and ecclesiastical construction as equally worthy. Orderic's priority was to go travelling and in 1317 he set off, "I crossed the sea and visited the countries of the unbelievers in order to win some harvest of souls." He made his way through Istanbul, Tabriz, Shiraz, Baghdad, then by sea to India, Sri Lanka, Sumatra, Java, Borneo and China. His account of his route back overland from Beijing to Venice is brief and patchy, but it was then, around 1328, that he visited Tibet. Back in Italy in 1330 he dictated his story to another friar, William of Solagna, before dying from the strain of his journey a year later. His death so soon after arriving back from these exotic adventures led to a huge outpouring of popular devotion. At his burial in Udine, crowds tried to touch and kiss the hands and feet of the corpse and snatch off pieces of clothing as relics. A week later he was exhumed and reburied in order to satisfy the wishes of the gentry to be present at this important occasion.

Today he is a saint and his body is interned in the Church of San Pedro in Udine. It is revealed on every fourth recurrence of his festival and is apparently still perfectly preserved, except for one leg, which has been frittered away in relics.

Recent commentators have doubted the truth of some of some of Orderic's claims. In a collection of writings compiled in the nineteenth century his travels are described as "a most superficial relation and full of lies... In short, it seems plain from the names of places and other circumstances that he never was in those countries (China and Tartary) but imposed on the public the few informations he had from others, mixed with many fictions of his own." The index of the same collection refers to Orderic as "A great liar."[3] However, if he came back from China overland, then there is every chance that he crossed Tibet. Many of the Silk Road traders at that time were enterprising Tibetans and, in order to travel safely, Orderic would have had to attach himself to a commercial caravan which might very well have passed through Tibet (and maybe even Lhasa).

Another criticism levelled at Orderic was that he was not a particularly devoted friar; he enjoyed roving and exploring too much to settle down for long and do serious missionary work. This seems justified - the only place he seems to have preached was Beijing, otherwise he was more interested in moving around and seeing the exotic sites of the Orient. Yet, this shortcoming as a friar is one of the attractions of Orderic as a travel writer. His account is wide-ranging and eclectic with an interest in the bizarre that is entertaining: He was fascinated by the Sumatrans who went naked all day, held their women in common and eagerly devoured human flesh (particularly children, brought to the islands by traders). He entitles another whole chapter "Concerning a certain melon that produceth a beast like a lamb." He was not a scholar like many of his fellow Franciscans who were coming to dominate the European Universities. If he were to read anything today it would be a tabloid (maybe he would even write for one).

What fascinated him most of all in Tibet was the process of sky burial, the method where the body is cut up and fed to

---

[3] Quoted by Henri Cordier in notes to "The Travels of Friar Orderic." Orderic of Pordenone, translated by Henry Yule, Hakluyt Society 1916.

vultures (a subject which amply satisfied his taste for the sensational.)

"And another fashion they have in this country is this. Suppose one's father were to die, then the son will say, "I desire to pay respect to my father's memory"; and so he calls together all the priests and monks and players in the country, and likewise all the neighbours and kinsfolk. And they carry the body into the country with great rejoicings. And they have a great table in readiness, upon which the priests cut off the head, and then this is presented to the son. And the son and all the company raise a chant and make many prayers for the dead. Then the priests cut the whole body to pieces, and when they have done so they go up again to the city with the whole company, praying for him as they go. After this the eagles and vultures come down from the mountains and every one takes his morsel and carries it away. Then all the company shout aloud, saying, "Behold! The man is a saint! For the angels of God come and carry him to Paradise…" He takes his father's head, and straightway cooks and eats it; and of the skull he maketh a goblet, from which he and all of the family always drink devoutly to the memory of the deceased father." [4]

Tibetan sky burial is still practised widely today (although the cannibalistic element that Orderic describes is not and probably never was a part of the ceremony.) Sky burials have a practical as well as a spiritual rationale. In a land of shallow soil, sanitary burial is difficult and would be a waste of scarce agricultural land. Corpses would also take a long time to decompose in the dry and cold environment of the plateau. Cremation is equally impractical as wood and dung are valuable

[4] Ibid.

and rare commodities, and certainly not available in large enough quantities for funeral pyres.

I had not planned to see a sky burial as I had been warned that, quite justifiably, Tibetans find the presence of curious tourists at their funerals insulting. However we were now sharing our dormitory with Paul, a fifty year old tour guide from Glastonbury, a part time grave digger and a new age dowsing teacher. Sky burials fascinated him and he had a note in his passport that instructed if he should die in Tibet he should receive a sky burial. He had already bought a drinking cup in the market made from a human cranium carved with the auspicious swastika. He had visited several sky burial sites and told us it was not offensive to visit as long as we kept away when they were actually cutting up bodies. "We wouldn't want people watching our burials, but we wouldn't mind them visiting our graveyards," was the way he justified it.

Simon claimed to be taking the immobile approach to acclimatisation (I think he was more put off by the 7 o'clock start) and spent the day in Lhasa, while I went with Paul to the sky burial site at Ganden monastery, two hours away. As the bus rolled through the desolate flood plain of the Lhasa River we talked. Paul had done archaeology at Cambridge back in the late sixties and had taken odd jobs after graduation, chiefly grave digging, or "archaeology in reverse" as he called it. He had become involved in a biker gang, The Wolves, and proudly showed me the wolf tattoo on his forearm. Years of drugs, fighting and a spell in prison had followed. He had now settled down and was pursuing his academic interests in Glastonbury: a sourcebook on Glastonbury's monastic history and an introduction for what he thought was the first British lesbian novel. I told him how I had fallen into banking straight after university, and fallen out just as quickly a couple of years later. His reaction was, "Yeah I imagine joining a biker gang is not such a popular choice for graduates these days…"

The bus strained up the twisting road to Ganden and passed the cluster of monastic buildings, lying under the ruins of others on the hill above, left after the Chinese battered the monastery into submission forty years before. We followed the other Tibetans as they set off round the hill to make their ritual Kora. Towards the end of the circuit we saw the sky burial site, a bare stone platform slightly beneath the path. Paul's eyes lit up, "Come on Iain, lets have a gander." It looked deserted but I was still nervous of clumsily walking in on a group of grieving relatives. However, the only people we came across were two young boys with sling shots which they demonstrated for us, sending stones flying into the sky with a "thwack" and a "whirr."

The platform itself was made of rocks held together with concrete. All around was the equipment for the sky burial process. A brazier for burning the hair, rusty knives and a small hatchet for hacking up the body, and a large, round, dark stone used for popping open the skull so that the brains could be disposed of. The instruments were lying haphazardly, covered with a brown residue that I hoped was just rust. Piles of what looked like abandoned clothes lay in heaps around the platform, and silk scarves were caught in the bushes flapping like trapped ghosts. From the site we could see the whole flood plain stretched below us in myriad shades of grey and on the hills opposite the green horizontal stitches of field terraces, nurtured with channelled water and yak dung. High up in the sky two vultures had appeared, and glided around us in wide circles - drawn by the presence of humans on the platform, which presumably normally signalled feeding time.

Paul insisted on a photo of him lying spread-eagled on the slab as if he was about to be hacked up. "You know I had the strangest sensation lying back there," he said earnestly as he walked back towards where I stood with his camera. "I closed my eyes and had a vision of a great red line, then when I opened them a vulture was the first thing I saw. Very weird feeling. Bit scary." He was right; the place had an eerie feel about it. I couldn't help being squeamish about the scattered butcher's equipment. Less grisly but somehow more sinister were the piles of clothes, left behind as if the dead had recently shrugged them off and stepped off the earth.

On the path above us I could see the two boys whirling their slings and sending stones spinning into the air as they tried to hit the wheeling vultures.

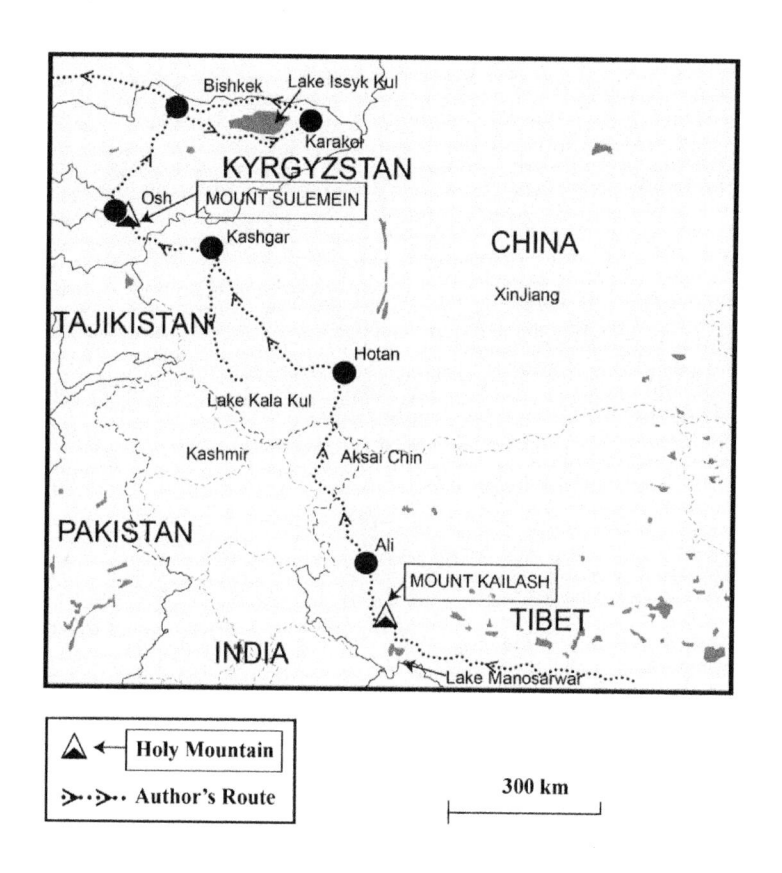

Map showing the author's route through Kyrgyzstan, China (Xinjiang), and Tibet, with locations including Bishkek, Lake Issyk Kul, Karakol, Osh, Mount Sulemein, Kashgar, Hotan, Lake Kala Kul, Kashmir, Aksai Chin, Ali, Mount Kailash, and Lake Manosarwar.

CHAPTER 3

To Kailash

The metalled road stopped on the outskirts of Lhasa and our wheels sent up an opaque plume of dust as we rattled along the main track west. Every time we passed a truck coming in the opposite direction we frantically wound up the windows, before we were engulfed in their dust trail. Too slow and the dust exploded through the gap, settling in a fine film on the dashboard and the back of my throat.

There were six of us squeezed into the Land Cruiser. The boot was stuffed with provisions and two cans of petrol were lashed to the roof rack. It felt good to be moving towards Kailash at last. After our bad experience of Chinese travel bureaucracy I had been dreading the results of our second permit application but everything had gone smoothly. We were held up for an hour while Sandra treated our hotel owner for his deafness with her homeopathic pills, then we were roaring away through the polythene covered fields around Lhasa.

The road headed along the Lhasa River before cutting into the valley of the Tsangpo River, which blasted through steep, fractured banks. Prayer flags fluttered hopefully from the girders of temporary-looking metal bridges that crossed the indentations of the Tsangpo's tributaries. Where these streams entered the river there was a brief ellipse of clear water, before they were swallowed up in the brown slurry of the main river.

In Assam the Tsangpo flattens and its name changes to the Brahmaputra; it becomes wide and flat but in Tibet it has the angry energy of youth, churning and roiling in waves, tumbling down gorges and eating away at the banks that contain it. We spent all day following its course upstream before cutting up onto high plains, where uninterrupted, smooth dunes of fine dust rolled all the way to the distant folds of mountains.

It was dark when we pulled into Shigatse, Tibet's second city, 250 kilometres south-west of Lhasa, where we were installed in a barrack-like guesthouse. Our driver and guide began their familiar routines. Sonawangde was the driver, a small figure with wisps of wire wool hair on a strangely compressed head. He smoked constantly as he drove but now he put out his cigarette and clambered over the engine to stick his arm deep into the machinery. He pulled out the carburettor, dribbling petrol and tapped it onto a rock then blew into the end sending spurts of rust-coloured fluid out. "Bad petrol," he explained. Turning it round he sucked the gritty fluid into his mouth before spitting. He repeated this process several times, refilling the distributor with a can of petrol, until the sediment was washed away and the petrol ran clear. He washed his mouth out with green tea before lighting another cigarette.

While Sonawangde got on with his unpleasant maintenance job, our official guide, Norgay, latched onto the young assistant hotel manageress and pulled her onto his knee where she laughed coquettishly and played with his baseball cap. Norgay was thirty years old and unmarried - a Lhasa bachelor who was enjoying his life on the road. A bed was made up for Norgay in our dormitory but he didn't sleep in it that night. The next day he was dead tired and dozed in the front seat with his baseball cap pulled over his eyes while we continued west.

*

For four days we drove, Sonawangde crouched over the wheel, Norgay, cap on backwards, sleeping or replaying the same two tapes of Tibetan pop over and over again. At each checkpoint he would straighten his cap and assume a serious expression while our reams of permits were stamped by the military or the PSB or the TTB or whoever ran that particular checkpoint.

The flatness gave way to tight river valleys where the crumbling sides ran in bands of red, yellow and grey and the water fed bushes with neon blue flowers, like electric heather. The track wound up towards passes, the tops marked by regiments of cairns each one alight with strings of wind-whipped prayer flags. Beyond the flags, more hours of straight road and plateau. Sometimes hidden, sometimes far on the horizon beckoned the shining promise of the snow covered peaks.

At night we stopped in lonely villages like Sunsuang, nestling in the lee of the hills with the expanse of the plateau beyond, flat and featureless, punctuated only by the black spots of yak and tzo (half yak, half cow) grazing far into the distance. I sketched the scene before it got dark, gathering a small crowd of children who watched every movement of my pen. One toddler was so mesmerised by the movement of pen on paper that he peered closer and closer until he overbalanced and fell onto me. His sister pulled him away and shouted at him until he went off crying with his finger comfortingly up his nose.

I was sitting on a small mound overlooking the village when the sun finally sank behind the mountains and the cold crept in with the shadow. Lights came on in the crevice-like windows of the houses and the dogs cried out warnings into the dark. What had been inconspicuous, dozing piles of fur during the day awoke with vicious energy and began asserting their territory. I stumbled down the mound to the guesthouse but I had been noticed by a grey dog, which started barking ferociously and bounded towards me. I remember being told the best way to scare off dogs was by crouching to pick up a stone. Even if one has no intention of throwing it, dogs soon learn to recognise this crouching-for-a-stone movement and scamper away. This had worked for me with angry Peruvian sheep dogs, it had worked with Highland Collies, but it had no effect on this Tibetan beast. It continued its advance to within a few feet of me barking crazily until I scurried into the guest house.

*

It rained on our third day of driving, and we became stuck on a deeply rutted track, thick with loamy mud. For miles around there was only short grass and wet earth; nothing that we could use to give the wheels purchase on the track. Engaging the four-wheel drive made no difference, all four wheels simply dug themselves in deeper, spraying cold slurry onto the windows. We sat in the jeep for half an hour until a truck arrived, and pulled us free on a steel cable.

All day the road got worse. When it was dry we threw up clouds of dust but the going was quick; when it rained the heavy soil kept the water sitting in large dark puddles for days. Then the road split into many tracks like an unravelled rope, as each successive driver strayed from the road to avoid the puddles and find firmer ground.

When we got stuck mid-river, Sonawangde had to get out in his black leather slip-ons and engage the four-wheel drive with a spanner, while water ran around his knees, his cigarette still clamped between his teeth. He was still smiling when he got back in, despite having soaked trousers, and shoes that squeaked against the rubber of his pedals. Sonawangde never stopped smiling. On a tough bit of road he might wince and give a quiet groan, but these seemed to be in sympathy with the straining engine, rather than from any personal frustration and when over the worst he always gave his squashed smile. The only serious problem we had was when the exhaust fell off on our third day of driving. Sonawangde tied it to the towing hook with twine to stop it dragging along the ground and we continued, sounding like a speedway motorbike. Sonawangde knew of an isolated hut half an hour up the road where an old man appeared from a one-roomed shack with gas canisters and an oxy-acetylene torch and in a couple of hours the exhaust was welded back on.

Sometimes we would pass other jeeps, full of Chinese men in gold aviator shades, but there were not many other vehicles on the roads and mostly they were long trucks, always the same shade of blue, with white circles of stencilled Chinese characters on the doors. The biggest were the petrol tankers rumbling and rocking as they inched their way across the deeply rutted roads like prehistoric beasts. Trucks tended to travel in twos, working a buddy-buddy system, helping each other with repairs, pulling one another out of mud pools, and providing company on their long, lonely journeys.

The exhaust repairs had delayed us by three hours so it was dark when we stopped for the third night on the road. The guesthouse was locked up and it took five minutes of Norgay banging on the door before we were let in. Despite our arrival at such an anti-social hour, the Tibetan hostess still brought us thukpa (noodle soup) with a hunk of yak meat on the bone floating in the centre of each bowl. This was followed with elderly yoghurt, which had gone fizzy and tasted of mature cheese.

A Chinese martial arts video badly dubbed into Tibetan was played for us as we ate. I wrote up my notes from the long day by its flickering light and tried to shut out the hysterical cries of kung-fu. It was still dark when we left, bleary eyed, the next morning for the final long day.

*

We were driving along a river valley, just another in the long progression of plateau and valley when the sky seemed to brighten; there was a sparkle and freshness in the air which felt like the seaside, the particular light caused by sun reflecting off a great expanse of water. As we climbed the lip at the end of the valley we saw it for the first time, a giant lake glittering in the low-lying sun like crumpled steel. Sonawangde and Norgay cheered "Lake Manosarwar," and Sonawangde took the jeep on an impromptu motor powered kora, clockwise around a low pile of stones festooned with prayer flags.

The wind was bitingly cold here where it blew uninterrupted across the water and we stood sheltering in the lee of the jeep. Sonawangde and Norgay lifted their hands in prayer, and prostrated themselves, silhouetted against the shining lake. Above the lake, and looking suddenly very close was the enormous bulk of Gurla Mandhata, vast and immovable, etched into the blue sky behind.

North towards the horizon, Norgay pointed to the mountain that we had come to visit, the distinctive outline of Kailash. Still small in the distance but unmistakable as it rose above the surrounding hills. This was the mountain I had first seen on the mandala of the exiled monk four years before. I thought of him now, his quiet words as he smoothed rolled pictures, which were cracked and dry. This was the long road he had taken towards India with Kailash behind him and paintings hidden in the folds of his clothing.

The snowfields on the ridged diamond shape of the south face were blazing white. I could just make out the sloping cross in high relief against the horizontal lines of rock where the snow did not lie. The Kailash massif is made from layers of sediment laid down thousands of years ago at the bottom of the ocean. These successive layers of compressed silt emerge today as the lines of a huge swastika on the side of the mountain (in this part of the world an auspicious Buddhist symbol rather than the sinister symbol it is in Europe).

Norgay pointed down at the sparkling water. "It was in this lake that Buddha's mother, Queen Maya bathed in a dream to wash before the Buddha's conception. The Buddha descended into her from the direction of Mount Kailash shaped as a white cloud elephant." He pointed beyond Manosarwar to the brackish lake of Rakshas Tal. "The connection between the lakes is the Ganga-cha. The lakes are like the sun and moon. It is said if water flows from one lake to the other lake along the Ganga-cha it is good news for Tibet. Now the water is flowing again. So many years dry – no water, but now there is flow. It is happy news for Tibet."

To celebrate the first sight of the mountain, Norgay gave us all small bitter blocks of chewing tobacco. Norgay and Sonawangde took silk scarves to the Buddhist monument, the chorten, tying them to the rocks where they waved hysterically in the wind that blew off the water. The fatigue of four days in the jeep dropped away as we set off again towards Darchen, the village at the base of the mountain.

"Twenty six times I have driven to Kailash," beamed Sonawangde. "And every time it makes me happy."

CHAPTER 4

The Kora

In the light of the morning, we realised Darchen was not a pretty place. Plastic litter clogged the central stream, caught between stones and slowly bleaching in the trickle of water. Rocks had been cleared away in places to create small pools where women scoured out their pots, leaving behind soap bubbles and yellow slicks of congealed butter on the surface. We crossed the stream on a slatted bridge, which wobbled and rocked, threatening to tip us into the filth.

Tents made up most of Darchen, housing the hordes of summer pilgrims. The canvas ridges had originally been white, but mud from the ground was slowly bleeding up the material, brown at the bottom, yellow at the top, like a large chromatography demonstration. The tents sat in circles of four or five along the side of the river, the worn rigging of guy ropes tangled about them. A few concrete buildings made up the core of the town, the government guest house, (extortionately priced, but compulsory for foreign tourists) the police offices, the petrol station and a long stinking latrine block.

We ate breakfast in one of the tents, where Tibetan tea was being made as we arrived. We watched the process: first chunks of tea leaf were flaked into boiling water. Next rancid yak butter, salt and bicarbonate of soda was added. The whole mixture was poured into a long wooden drum and vigorously churned until it had emulsified. It was served to us accompanied by tsampa, the staple Tibetan food of roasted barley flour. The trick to eating tsampa is to create moist balls by mixing the dry powder with a little tea (and preferably some sugar).

      Three monks sat opposite us in the breakfast tent; exhausted faces painted with sweat lines through dust. They had completed the Kailash Kora early that morning in one continuous twenty hour walk (it would take us three days). They poured butter tea over the top of their tsampa and licked at the dampened top layer, then laughed as they watched me spill the powder all over my knees while trying to mix it into a ball. Beside them lay their religious devotional objects, a little pair of cymbals, the symbolic thunderbolt, and a bell, which they passed for us to hold in our hands.

*

Norgay was meant to be guiding us round the mountain, but, despite eating plenty of tsampa for breakfast, he announced that he had eaten bad noodles the previous night and was feeling ill. He needed a day to recover, but said he would catch us up the next day at the first campsite by setting off at four in the morning. As we left, Norgay handed us apples and bottles of Chinese cola. "It is good luck to give gifts to someone leaving for the Kora."

   It was a relief to leave the squalor of Darchen. It looked better from the distance; a smattering of white tent roofs, each one sending out a thin line of smoke which slanted diagonally in the gentle morning wind. The path was hard packed and wide and we contoured the front of the mountain on the level.

Sometimes I tucked my hands into the shoulder straps, or held them behind my back, transferring the weight from my waist and shoulders to my arms. I sucked the air in, we were high, but I was breathing easily and enjoying the movement. Our party of three spread out, taking the walk at our own pace, enjoying the space and physical release after four days in the jeep.

To my left stretched miles of the Barkha Plain, interrupted only by a river, which meandered blindly across the middle. Manosarwar Lake was not visible from here but I could see the white shoulders of Gurla Madhata towering above it. Mountains surrounded us. Further to the west were the twin peaks of Kamet, pointing away from one another like thick horns. Still further round, almost in front of me, the bulk of Nanda Devi marked the border with India, its base invisible as the earth curved away from me, but its upper few thousand metres sticking straight out of the plain, white against brown.

The path cut right, away from the plain into Amitabha, The Red Valley, where scarred russet cliffs dwarfed the meandering lines of pilgrims. It had been dark as we approached the mountain the previous night and we had been too close to the foothills to see its summit when we woke that morning. So it was for the first time that we saw Kailash close-to as we rounded the last line of cliffs and came upon the fin-like western face. At the base the ground looked as if it had been piled up in giant handfuls and still bore the ridges and furrows of its formation. Above, the rock had been eroded into unlikely waves and curves, shot over by the shadows of cracks and faults. The icy pyramid continued in equilateral lines until the smooth white summit, blemished only by evenly spaced horizontal etchings of sedimentary rock that poked through the snow pack. I sat beside the path and gazed at this display of dominance and elegance and understood that this was a place where Gods could live.

*

In the Hindu epics, the Puranas, the centre of the cosmos and birthplace of the world is Mount Meru, a mountain whose four sides are made of crystal, ruby, gold and lapis and which is protected from the peripheral worlds by great mountain ranges. The river Ganges flows down this mythical mountain and splits into four rivers, which go to the four corners of the earth. The pyramid shaped Kailash, lying as it does on the other side of the Himalayas from India, and whose glaciers were said to feed four great rivers of Asia, was the obvious earthly manifestation of Meru for the Indians of the Punjab. The iconic image of the mountain at the centre of the world was spread far and wide in the Hindu epics and in the devotional paintings that the Hindus called yantras and the Buddhists mandalas, which showed Meru at the centre of the cosmos.

Then, as geographical knowledge increased and it became apparent that there really was a perfect pyramid shaped mountain beyond the Himalaya, which fed the four rivers of the subcontinent, the cult of the mythical Mount Meru transferred to the real Mount Kailash. As I had been told several years earlier: *It is Mount Meru in heaven and Kange Rinpoche in Tibet.*

Hindu belief places Shiva, the transformer and destroyer and the god of mountains on top of Kailash where he spends his time practising yogic austerities and making love with his female counterpart, Devi. Tibetan Buddhists call the mountain Kange Rinpoche (Precious Snow Mountain) and believe the summit is occupied by the wrathful Demokog, the four-faced demon armed with trident and drum, and his female counterpart Dorje Phangmo. The Jains[5] call it Astapada and believe that the first of their twenty-four Jinas (spiritual victors), called Rishaba, was emancipated through devotion to the five Jain vows on the mountain. The Bonnists[6] believe that the sacred Yungdrung Gutseg (the Bonnist name for Kailash, which means Nine Swastika Mountain) was where the Bonnist founder Shenrab alighted from heaven. They believe that the Bon goddess Sipaimen resides on the summit.

As the meeting place of these varied religions, it is fitting that Kailash should be the setting for a legendary Tibetan spiritual contest that symbolised the struggle between the new religion, Buddhism, and the incumbent Tibetan Bonnist religion in the seventh century. The legend goes that Yogi Milarepa, the champion of Tantric Buddhism, and Naro-Bonchung, the champion of the shamanistic Bonnism, went to battle over who should be allowed to claim Kailash for their own. After a battle of magic spells they agreed that whoever reached the top of the mountain first would be the winner of the contest. The Bonnist master Naro-Bonchung began flying early in the morning, making steady progress towards the triangular peak dressed in a green cloak, playing a thighbone trumpet and sitting on his shamanistic drum. Milarepa, the

---

[5] Jainism is an ancient Indian religious and philosophical tradition, which derives its name from Jinas (spiritual victors) the title given to the twenty-four great teachers. The aim of Jain spiritual endeavour is to liberate the soul by freeing it from accumulated karma, by following five vows: non-injury, speaking the truth, not taking anything not given, chastity and detachment from place, persons and things.

6 Bonnism is the animist, shamanistic non-literate religion of Tibet, present before the arrival of Buddhism in Tibet in the seventh century.

Buddhist, distressed his supporters by remaining asleep until the very last moment when he suddenly soared towards the summit at an incredible speed, overtaking the Bonnist. In his shock at the power of his Buddhist adversary the Bonnist dropped his drum, which is said to have caused the vertical gash down the South face of Kailash (the line which makes up the upright stroke of the swastika). The Buddhist yogi won the contest and took his place on top of Kailash expelling Naro-Bonchung to a smaller mountain to the East. It was Buddhism which came to dominate religious life in Tibet while Bonnism was relegated to a minority position. As with Emei Shan, the great mountains of Asia have become the canvas for folk tales that tell us about the memories and preoccupations of those who live among them.

The beliefs and practises of Bonnism are now heavily influenced by Buddhist ideology and although the religion retains a definite shamanistic element it would probably be unrecognisable to the Bonnists of pre-Buddhist Tibet. So much has the old religion metamorphosed that in 1998 the Dalai Llama formally accepted the body of beliefs as one of the five schools of Tibetan Buddhism. Bonnists today continue to be devoted to Mount Kailash and make koras of the mountain, despite their mythical loss. They are only distinguishable because they make the circuit in an anti-clockwise direction, the opposite way from the Buddhists.

Kailash stands at only 6,700m and is not a technically difficult climb, but to those who revere the peak as the abode of their gods, the idea of a mortal climbing it is anathema. The Chinese authorities granted permission for the famous Italian mountaineer Reinhold Messner to climb it in the 1980s but he abandoned the attempt in deference to the peak's sanctity and instead performed the Kora at a record speed. In May 2001 a group of Spanish climbers gained permission to climb the peak but also abandoned their attempt in the face of international protests. To this day the only mortal who is said to have reached the top and seen the gods on the summit is the twelfth century flying monk, Yogi Milarepa.

*

Halfway up the Red Valley we reached Tarboche, where every year around mid-April, to celebrate Buddha's ascent to Nirvana, the Saga Dawa festival takes place. At Kailash the celebrations involve the raising of a giant flagpole festooned with prayer flags. Amid carnival scenes the pole is pulled up by teams of men (and nowadays trucks), using a complicated arrangement of ropes and foundation rocks. It is vital that the flagpole is absolutely vertical, as if it is off centre then it is believed to be a sign of bad luck for Tibet for the next year.

Lines of prayer flags are hung around the pole, and in long sloping lines tied at intervals up the pole, so that a giant cone of flapping flags is created, echoing the shape of the peak behind.

Trucks dropped off their loads of pilgrims and their luggage at Tarboche as many Tibetans begin their Kora here rather than at Darchen. We had seen a few of these people-carrying trucks on our way across the plateau: trussed up sacks and boxes were heaped on the truck bed with the passengers clinging-on on top, legs dangling over the edge. It was a long, bitterly cold ride and the passengers concealed themselves in layers of bulky clothes, balaclavas and dust masks, leaving hardly any bare skin visible. The previous night we had passed one of these over-laden trucks in the darkness stuck in boggy ground, with half the passengers dismounted, pushing and shouting at the driver. As it lurched from one puddle to the next, the passengers pursued it whooping. They all wore the thick dressing-gown-like garments called chubas and the men had swords hanging from their belts; in the darkness they looked like they were engaged in the heroic hunt for some growling mythic beast.

There was a feeling of closeness among the pilgrims at Tarboche; for them something very special was being shared. Those who had just finished the kora, wandered around with glazed eyes and flushed cheeks, still sweating with exertion, their chubas hanging in voluminous folds from their waists. Those who had yet to start were still cold from their journey and hobbled with stiff legs as they made their initial Kora around the flagpole. They could not contain their excitement about their imminent departure and hailed the arriving pilgrims with questions.

A father tied and retied his son's shoelaces and used the sleeve of his chuba to wipe the boy's nose. Loads were pulled from the collage of packages and distributed among the extended family groups. Babies were stowed in thickly wrapped bundles on their parents backs, and hung, only their faces exposed, looking backwards or sideways in completely immobile little parcels.

*

The eradication of the sins of a lifetime through the devotional circumambulation of the holy mountain symbolises the passage of an entire lifetime during the walk. The Kora begins with a symbolic death and halfway round on the highest pass the pilgrims sins are wiped away with a symbolic rebirth. Just after

Tarboche is the point where the death takes place, which the pilgrims mark by discarding a piece of clothing or parts of livestock at the arched Chorten Kangnyi.

It is a gruesome sight. Beside the piles of clothing, pilgrims have tied goats' heads and strings of goat knuckles to the entrance of the passageway. In the cold dry air the goats' heads are slow to rot, and they hang, eyeless but still red-crusted where they have been separated from the body. I push through this grisly curtain into the passage, where the walls are lined with more skulls and the floor completely covered with pieces of clothing and more severed goats' heads, which crack as I step on them. Outside a grinning pilgrim is tying a string of yaks' vertebrae to the collection.

Above the Chorten is the sky burial site. This particular site, on a rocky shelf on the lower reaches of Kailash is one of the most auspicious burial sites in Tibet, the burial site of the "Eighty Four Enlightened Ones." Unlike the relatively tidy site at Ganden that I had visited from Lhasa, this site looked messy as if the sky burials had taken place with undue haste. I didn't hang around; I felt a terrible combination of squeamishness and the self-conscious suspicion that I was some sort of voyeuristic gore-tourist by even looking in the direction of the platform.

"I'm not sure you want to go up there," I told Simon as I met him coming up the track, but, of course, he did, and returned a few minutes later looking pale. We continued walking in silence.

*

In the clear air I could see far along the wide half pipe of the glacial valley where pilgrims marched in meandering lines like ants. Now that they had warmed up, the men had dropped the top of their chubas from their shoulders so that the whole garment hung from their waists like a clumsy bustle. They carried very little in the way of equipment, and their few blankets or provisions were stuffed in the folds of their chubas, or slung across one shoulder in a worn fabric fertiliser bag tied at the neck and one corner with nylon twine. They called out to us as we passed "Hallo, Hallo, Tashi Delli," and posed in elaborate family groups for photographs. The Swedish explorer, Sven Hedin, the first European to make the Kailash Kora (in 1907) described his fellow pilgrims:

"I saw the silent procession, the faithful bands, youths and maidens, strong men with wife and child, grey old men, ragged fellows who lived like parasites on the charity of other pilgrims, scoundrels who had to do penance for a crime, robbers who had plundered peaceful travellers, chiefs, officials, herdsmen and nomads; a varied train of shady humanity on the thorny road, which after interminable ages ends in the peace of Nirvana. August and serene, Siva looks down from his paradise, and Hlabsen from his jewelled palace, on the innumerable human beings below who circle like asteroids in the sun, round the foot of the mountain."

It felt good to be walking with the locals. Something I always noticed when trekking among the spectacular peaks of India and South America was that you were doing something completely inexplicable to the people who lived there who tended to regard you with a mixture of pity and bemusement. For them it was a chore or a job to trudge up to the high pastures and do the milking or bring down the goats; westerners who sweated along the very same tracks with huge multicoloured rucksacks for fun were clearly quite mad (or up to no good.) Such incomprehension necessarily puts a certain distance between the tourist and the local. It felt different on the Kailash Kora. We were all doing the same thing, just walking round a mountain and little distinction was made whether we were doing it for pleasure or curiosity or for karma.

To gain extra merit some pilgrims prostrate themselves for the whole Kora. They clap their hands together in front of them, then lie down on their fronts with their arms stretched as far as they could go. Then they get up and walk to the spot where their hands reached, which they mark with a stone or a shell and repeat the whole process again, all the way around the mountain. They wear gym shoes or wooden blocks held on by string on their hands and large rubber or leather aprons, so that on a flat path they can launch themselves with a leap and slide an extra couple of feet. Later we would see these committed pilgrims prostrating themselves onto snowfields, and even crossing streams flat on their stomachs. At night they mark the spot they have reached and walk to the nearest monastery to sleep. A prostrating Kora takes two to three weeks, but repays its efforts by being equivalent to thirteen conventional circambulations of the mountain.

Often the prostraters that we saw were boys and girls in their early teens, who looked dirty and exhausted. It was a painful way of acquiring merit and at first I felt slightly repelled by the emphasis on what seemed like pointless physical discomfort. It reminded me of the medieval craze of self-flagellation. However, this reaction misunderstood these prostrating pilgrims – their motivation was not simply to mortify the body. In the same way that pilgrims took home stones and pinches of earth from the mountain in the belief that physical contact with part of the mountain harnessed its power, the main aim of lying on the ground all the way round the circuit was to absorb Kailash's power. The Dalai Llama has explained this, "When you walk a circular pilgrimage route, such as this one around Mount Kailash, your feet touch the earth with big spaces between them, but when you prostrate, your whole body connects with the sacred ground to close the circle."[7] A prostrating Kora was not about pain and discomfort but about an intimacy of contact with the mountain.

*

At the end of the valley we realised we had overshot Diru-puk monastery, the last campsite before the high pass, and were forced into a numbing barefoot river crossing. Dira-Puk monastery consisted of only a couple of rooms, built around a cave shrine in the cliff. The entrance to the shrine was a narrow crack in the rock, and we waited in line with the other visitors to crawl in and look at the holy figures in a flickering lamplight. The air inside the cave was humid and thick with the sweet, cloying, and now familiar, smell of yak butter from the sputtering lamps. We were jostled and shunted by the bodies of other pilgrims with a sense of friendly familiarity that is an integral part of the Tibetan religious experience.

We had been told that there would be big tents put up to accommodate pilgrims at Dira-Puk but the monks told us that this late in the year they had all been taken down. They invited us to sleep on the monastery floor but it was already crowded and we had brought bivouac bags with us in case we had to sleep outside. We walked down to the flat shelf of the

---

[7] "The Cult of Pure Crystal Mountain," Toni Huber, Oxford University Press, 1999.

riverbank where the tents had been pitched and built a low wall to give our bivouac site some shelter. Then we rested, panting from the exertion of moving rocks at this altitude. Above us was the North face of Kailash, by far the most spectacular of the faces. Here the pyramid had been shattered leaving a sheer vertical face, opaquely veined like the wing of an insect and overshadowed with the curling lips of cornices running all the way around the summit ridge. The evening sun shone through a brief snowstorm on the top and the mountain glowed orange. The colour spread from the clouds to the plastering of snow and for a moment the mountain was on fire.

I slurped down our dinner of noodles and yak cheese and wished I had brought more cheese, as it was the only food of any real substance that we had with us. The noodles were full of strange chemicals that just seemed to bloat our stomachs and loosen our bowels. Each flavour, beef and chilli, chicken and lemon, clam and ginger, tasted exactly the same. We got sick of them quickly, and wished we had not decided to rely on them for every meal.

We heated water to drink but the chlorine in the water purifiers made it taste like drinking from a swimming pool. Our fire of dried yak dung and paper from my diary burned pathetically in the thin air then went out. The sun sank behind dark foothills, the temperature dropped and there was nothing for us to do but put on all our clothes, cocoon ourselves in sleeping bags, bivouac bags and our empty rucksacks and lie immobile in a line behind our little wall. The cold woke me at intervals in the night seeping through the layers of nylon and fleece like water. When a light dusting of snow fell I pulled the orange plastic of the bag over my face and listened to it patter on the outside.

Dawn broke at 7:30, sunlight hitting the top of Kailash and rapidly spreading down the whole face, an ochre wash replacing the blue light of the moon. We stayed huddled in our bags watching the warmth of the sun crawl slowly along the ground. On the other side of the river, the streams of pilgrims were already in full flow on their one-day Kora, having started at Darchen or the Tarboche just after midnight. They would reach the top of the pass before the sun got too strong and would be back in Darchen by evening. There was a biblical quality to the scene as lines and lines of figures passed beneath the face of this glowing mountain. We quickly joined them; our breakfast of slithering noodles being nothing to linger over.

We were soon climbing up steep ground to the Dorma La, the highest pass on the Kora at 5,630m. The easy valley walking of the previous day was replaced with a lung-ripping crawl up a steep path. I walked beside a shopkeeper from Lhasa for some time and he fired questions at me which I tried to answer between gasps. "What your country? What animals you have in your country? Tigers? Elephants? Camels? Yak? Sheep? You have mountains? How big?" It must have sounded a boring place to live. He told me he was making his tenth Kailash Kora. After three more Koras he would be permitted to undertake the inner Kora, a more meritorious route that nestles close to the mountain on steeper paths. However, the inner Kora is only open to those who have already proved their devotion to the mountain by undertaking thirteen conventional circuits.

This year was very special for him: it was the year of the water horse. Tibetans align each year with one of twelve animals, which are additionally connected with one of the five elements. This means that each type of year only comes around every sixty years. Each holy mountain is also aligned with an animal, in Kailash's case the horse and making a pilgrimage to the mountain during this auspicious year is judged to be especially powerful. "That is why there are so many pilgrims this year. *Very* lucky year."

Above the snow line the sun was dazzling. Many of the pilgrims did not have sunglasses and resorted to strips of fabric or a lock of their own hair tied around their eyes to cut out the glare. The wind dropped and I panted in the heat. Counting my steps, I pushed myself to reach forty before stopping to suck in air, taking longer to recover each time. The earth was dragging at my feet and the air catching in my throat like smoke. My steps got smaller so that I reached the forty more quickly, then I justified my longer rests by allowing myself a rest *after* I had stopped panting. A group of four women with elaborate domed hats and bunches of bells on their costumes passed me at a ferocious pace, the lightness of their step emphasised by the quick jingle of their bells. The noise of their laughter and bells left me as they accelerated into the distance and I was left with my own wheezes again, and the ever-slowing crunch of my footsteps on snow.

I seethed with frustration at yet another false summit, which in Tibet are especially believable as they are covered with cairns and prayer flags just like the real summits. Simon caught up with me as I tried to moisten the dry patch at the back of my throat with more nauseating chlorine flavoured water. He refused to pose with Kailash behind him because it involved, "unnecessary steps." Below us we could see Julia taking small, slow, constant steps. We would wait for her at the top. We trudged on together in the muddied snow of the path. The fatigue I felt and the sheer effort of moving is something I have only ever experienced before in a dream. I watched my legs bend and stumble sluggishly but even with these small, slow movements my lungs complained at unreasonable exertion.

At last the pass appeared, an eruption of prayer flags, and thin wreaths of aromatic smoke rising from burning bunches of juniper in the sheltered alcoves of altars. This was the high point of the Kora, the symbolic rebirth, and the absolution from the sins of a lifetime. But it was a painful absolution and at that moment I felt no relief. We slumped down on the snow, exhausted. Next to us three generations of a family were resting. The boy cannot have been more than six and was dressed in a thick woolly chuba with Chinese gym shoes on his feet. He regarded me, unblinking, snot-nosed and expressionless. His mother wore an elaborate hat, made of perfect brown fur with huge earflaps that bobbed up and down as though spring-loaded. A baby's face peered out, all but hidden in the wrappings which made up the formless bundle on the mother's back. The grandmother was busy unwrapping blocks of crunchy tsampa mixed with honey and cheese and passing them round the family. She saw me and held out one of the blocks towards me. I smiled and shook my head; the altitude was still suppressing my hunger. She gestured again, holding it out to me, then got up and walked over to me, thrusting it into my hand. In my jacket pocket I found one of the apples that Norgay had given to me and gave it to the little boy, who immediately bit into it.

We waited for Julia to arrive, but it had started snowing and we were getting cold – we would have to move on. The groups of pilgrims were packing up and the burning juniper fizzed and went out as the flakes landed on it. There was more snow on the other side of the pass. In the shadow of the mountain it had drifted deeply into the rut of the path.

We slithered down it, passing pilgrims who had let their long sleeves roll over their hands for warmth. We passed a group of about twenty Gore-tex clad Californian Buddhists on the Kora with their "spiritual leader." This was a well catered-for expedition, with one guide between two Californians. "Kailash rocks," grinned a bearded Californian in matching North Face jacket, salopettes, and ear warmers, as we passed him. Some of the older members were having difficulty as the path crossed a long boulder field, but there were plenty of guides to help out and some were leading the ageing Buddhists down the path by hand. Their luggage was carried by a long train of yaks and porters who overtook them during the day so that their tents and dinner were ready for their arrival in the evening. An hour later we passed their camp and were amazed by the industrial sized gas canisters, the picnic benches, and the *two* toilet tents. I counted twenty-five yaks grazing by the campsite, released from their loads for the night.

The air was thicker but my back and legs ached as we plodded on down the valley towards Zutul-Puk monastery. My rucksack pulled at shoulders too exhausted to support it. I felt weak and sick. We were silent as we trudged, stumbling when there were rocks in the path, utterly exhausted. For two hours a pale yellow dog, that looked a bit like a Labrador followed at my heels. It had a clean coat and while the other dogs on the mountain were badly tousled and scarred, this dog only had one scar under its left eye, that made me think of a noble Viennese duelling scar. It kept looking up the slope to the peak on our right and I imagined it a high lama reincarnated as a dog for some unspeakable sin, repeatedly doing koras of Kailash in penance - following pilgrims so as not to attract attention.

I had other strange thoughts too. I had picked up two green rocks from a cairn at the first campsite. Now I felt I shouldn't have and when I found another cairn I set them on top. It was unlike me. I saw myself, not as a sceptic, but certainly not as a prospective buddhist convert. I didn't have a devotion to any particular religion. But the process of going higher than I had ever been before in my life, of pulling myself over that pass, the rythmic motion of one-foot-in-front-of-the-other had a powerful effect. I suppose it was similar to a religious-mystic practice; the chanting of Buddhist monks, the whirling of Muslim dervishes, the fasting of Christian ascetics. Even with my confirmed secularity I was affected on a level that made me think slightly differently – I thought dogs might not just be dogs and stones could be special.

It was evening when we reached Zutul-Puk monastery; we had been walking for nine hours. There was a bunkhouse beside it, which meant we did not have to bivouac again. It was almost dark, but we sat outside watching for Julia, feeling a bit guilty as we had all the food in our bags. She did not appear, so we decided that as a fellow American she must have stayed in the luxurious Californian camp and even got a little jealous. What feasts they would be having carried round the mountain by that herd of yaks.

On the floor, in the arc of yellow head-torch light lay a half-eaten pan of noodles, outside in the valley the dogs were beginning to howl. Lying on the lumpy mattress of the monastery guest-house I wrote in my diary with cold-stiffened fingers:

"Very tired and empty but not hungry. Cold and knackered. But despite this, at the foot of this holy mountain, there is no place I would rather be. The pilgrimage around this mountain is so literal and uncompromising. The symbolic death on the high pass felt so painful, it might have been real. The icy pyramid looks like heaven should, and I can almost believe we have come closer to nirvana." It was one of the most enthusiastic passages I wrote in my diary, lying on my bed in a state of exhaustion-induced elation.

*

Norgay appeared the next morning. He told us his stomach had kept him back another day, but he had recovered and walked all night, crossing the Dorma La in a snowstorm. Julia appeared twenty minutes later, walking along the path in her rubber boots. She had walked until it had got dark but had not reached the monastery or seen the Californian camp-site so had bivvied out for a second night on top of a boulder about a mile from Zutul-Puk. She was looking drawn and weary and walked with the loose gait of the exhausted. Simon and I felt terribly guilty about having left her behind and rushed around making her tea and noodles.

It was an easy last day and it took us only two hours to get back to Darchen. We walked alongside a group of about twenty Tibetans, the adults tramping ahead with bundles of blankets on their backs and sleeping babies in their arms and children in the rear, squabbling over a bottle of yellow Chinese cola. They were a group of families who were part of a small semi-nomadic tribe from a place Norgay had not heard of somewhere in the Chantang (northern plateau.) They had clubbed together to hire an open sided truck for the thirty-day return journey to Kailash, leaving behind two relatives to look after the flocks of yak and goat. All the women wore deep maroon robes with bands of pink, green and brown in the skirted section, their hair in long plaits tied together at their waists and inlaid with rocks of turquoise and silver coins. Round their necks they wore elaborate chunky jewellery - amber pendants and huge strings of beads made from lapis lazuli and coral. The men wore dark beige chubas trimmed with grey and black fur (the clan colours) and long swords hung from their waists and swung about their legs. I asked one of the group with a particularly impressive sword if it had ever been drawn in anger and he replied,

"Never on a Tibetan. Only on a foreigner." His jaw set, his face cold for a second, before breaking into a deep gravelly laugh.

"They are not for fighting really," Norgay chuckled, "they are for skinning yaks."

Their chubas and fur hats looked just the same as those worn by Tibetans in photographs taken by explorers in the nineteenth century. Only their footwear betrayed which century these Tibetans lived in: deteriorating trainers with global sports brands.

The trip was expensive for the families. They would be away from their farmlands for a long time, but Buddhism was at the very centre of the lives of these subsistence nomads. It was also the water horse year. "And now," the man with the large sword smiled as his gaze drifted over his children (still fighting over the yellow bottle), "My children are safe for this life…"

CHAPTER 5

West

We left Sarah at Darchen. She had ended up making the kora with the Californian group (we resisted the temptation to question the value of a kora undertaken with twenty five yaks). She had arranged to stay with them as they went into a brief retreat in one of the nearby monasteries. She seemed to have lost the irritability and tension that had made her a trying companion on the drive west and we parted on good terms. This was the best arrangement for us too as we did not have the problem of an undecided passenger when we made our bid to hitchhike west from Ali.

With the mountain at our back, we drove to Lake Manosarwar, which glowed petrol green in the afternoon sun. There was a guesthouse here with large square tiled baths fed by a thermal spring. The water was slightly too cold for comfort, but it was pleasant to be submerged again, and to wash off the grime of a week. I shivered as I dried myself – for economy of space I had only brought a hand towel with me. We huddled in the kitchen of the guesthouse and ate food we had brought from Lhasa, salty crackers, corned beef, yak cheese, tsampa. I felt cold now that my hair was wet and I had washed off the layer of insulating grease. Bathing is not popular in Tibet and I could understand why.

The real reason for Norgay's delay had become clear as we were packing the jeep to leave Darchen. A tearful Tibetan girl in tight brown velvet trousers had come to say goodbye to him. They had exchanged lingering embraces and she had given him a dried fish from Lake Manosarwar as a parting gift. "Sore stomach was it, eh, Norgay?" Simon began, "So, there's one in Lhasa, one in Shigatse, and now one in Darchen. A girl in every port. *And* you did the kora in twenty hours. You must be knackered." Norgay smiled sheepishly and waved at the weeping girl as we drove away. That evening around the kitchen fire Norgay told us that the most beautiful girls in all of Tibet are from the Kham, Eastern Tibet. They have fair, soft skin and wide eyes. That was where the weeping Darchen girl was from. Her parents had come to Darchen to open a restaurant tent catering for the crowds of pilgrims. In a couple more weeks they would pack up and make the long drive back home for the winter.

"But maybe I will see her next year. If I bring another group to Kailash, then maybe she will be here again…"
There was a combined sense of exhaustion and sadness for all of us, now that the excitement of the kora was over. There was also the unvoiced concern about the next stage; a nervousness about the prospect of hitchhiking illegally. I went down to the sulphurous lakeside to be alone, to think of things at home and wash my brittle socks.

*

On the shore of Manosarwar we met a group of Indian pilgrims. There were thirty of them travelling in a fleet of Land Cruisers with five Nepalese cooks. As we arrived, the cooks were laying out a buffet lunch in lines of stainless steel trays. They pressed us to join them and we needed little prompting. It smelled delicious.

As I write this my mouth waters again. After days eating rehydrated Chinese noodles and bland tsampa with glutinous butter tea, the aromatic Indian dishes were delicious. Two types of sambar, butter dal, spinach rissoles, tamarind chutney, and Alfonso mango pickle were all scooped up with crisp parathas and fresh steaming puri bread. Pudding was a vat of caramel coloured sweet rice, spiced with cinnamon and nutmeg and swimming with little chunks of coconut. They asked Norgay and Sonawangde to take platefuls but they eyed the coloured pots (and the Indians) with suspicion and declined the offer. I tried to persuade them to have a taste. After the stodginess of Tibetan cuisine it would be a revolutionary experience. I wanted to see their reaction at the complex flavours but they would not be swayed. Sonawangde smoked and Norgay returned to our jeep to nibble on his dried fish.

Manosarwar is holy to Hindus, occupying a central position in their body of beliefs. The Hindu religious book The Skanda Purana tells the story of the Rishis, the sons of Brahma, who travelled to Kailash to pray there for twelve years. High on the arid plain, there was no water for them to drink or wash in and it became difficult for them to continue their rituals. They prayed to Brahma to give them some relief.

"Then Brahma by a mental effort formed the holy lake of Manasa and the Rishis again engaged in mortification and prayer on Kailash and worshipped the golden ling [phallus – the symbol of Shiva] which rose from the midst of the waters of the lake."[8]

The lake is an outward manifestation of the mind of Brahma, the four-headed creator from whom everything comes and to whom everything will return. While Buddhists

---

[8] "A Mountain in Tibet," Charles Allen, Abacus 1984.

make circambulations of the lake, the Hindus have a strong tradition of bathing in holy rivers and continue this even in the 4,560m elevated lake. Their immersions were noticeably briefer than those I have seen undertaken by the faithful in Indian rivers.

Their spiritual leader was Guru Rada Krishna Sonni, a thin, bowed figure with a long white beard that curled all the way down to his navel. We had seen him plunge himself into the water when we arrived. He was thin and frail looking but his face with its deep-set eyes and long hooked nose had the intensity of a bird of prey. He looked every inch a religious leader as he wandered the courtyard; a saffron robe draped over his bare torso and loose white trousers rolled up to the knee. When I had first seen his slight shape I imagined him to be a contemplative, silent man but I was wrong. "I do not need to eat, you know," he informed me shrilly as he mashed up a puri with his fingers. "You do not need to eat either, you are made up of five elements only. I could stop eating tomorrow." He had made twenty-six koras, but from his emaciated body it looked as though he would be blown away on the Dolma La. Rada Krishna ignored Simon as he hovered around taking photographs, as if as a guru he was quite used to this level of interest.

"I am lucky. It is good fortune that I can visit this holy place." He enjoyed the puzzled look on my face, then proceeded. "Every year, the Indian government, the *Indian Central Government*, organises a lottery. And they agree with the Chinese that four hundred and fifty Indian people, with Indian passports can enter Tibet from Garhwal over the Unta Dura Pass and visit Kailash. But every Hindu wants to come here to the holy mountain and each year five thousand people apply. It is difficult therefore, is it not, to come here?"

"BUT," he continued, his finger pointing in the air like a preacher in full flow, (Simon's shutter clicked excitedly) "Four times, in four years I was chosen. FOUR TIMES, by a lottery. So, I am lucky with good fortunes. And this year, I come with this group, as a guide for them, *a spiritual guide*, and we come through Kathmandu this year, which is easier."

The route from Garhwal is a direct but difficult path, inaccessible to motor vehicles. It takes several days to walk from India to the Tibetan roadhead and the trek requires a horse and porters. However, since 1992, a route via Kathmandu has been open to Indians with no limit on numbers, although the overall cost of coming this way is higher. This has opened the way for enterprising Indian tour operators to bring well-heeled groups to the mountain of Shiva. While researching Kailash on the Internet I had come across one of these companies that claimed "now because of modern transport system, the path to salvation is no longer an isolated dream." It offered several different levels of tour but my favourite was the "Bollywood Special Tour," which squeezed the whole trip into ten days by flying through Nepal to the Western border with Tibet.

"Considering the busy schedule and time constraints of Bollywood film-stars, celebrities and bosses of corporate houses," it advertised, "*MountKailash.com* has developed a special program… And with acclimatisation and O2 support, you will make your way to Mount Kailash in easy pace, which seems to be amazing for you like in a Bollywood movie."

*

We celebrated Simon's birthday dinner in Moincer, a tiny town a day west of Manosarwar, which consisted of eight buildings crowded round a military checkpoint. After a meal of Thukpa we ordered several Lhasa beers and I gave Simon a bottle of Chinese rum that smelled of pear drops. Sonawangde seemed worried that we were actually considering drinking this and warned us against it with dramatic displays of the headaches and sickness that would result, but Norgay assured us he was exaggerating.

Julia gave him a balaclava in the 1940s style with pompom and hard peak, that he had been admiring in Darchen. Norgay and Sonawangde sent the serving boy out to buy silk scarves which they draped ceremonially around his neck. The boy was told to take a photo of this funny group – all of us red-faced from rum and sun, Simon in the centre with hat and multiple scarves like some prince regent, grinning his widest smile and holding a shot of rum aloft.

We spent all of the next day driving to Ali. A huge road building programme was under way to replace the mud tracks and endless fords of Western Tibet. Teams of ragged figures huddled against the wind, mixing concrete in plastic lined hollows beside the road. The concrete embankments set with stones like crazy paving, sloped steeply several metres up to the highway. Every few miles there were workers' tents, single layers of plastic fabric, stretched over rough wooden frames - a splash of artificial brightness in this monochromatic landscape.

Ali was a shock after weeks on dirt roads. Our hotel room had flush toilets, television, and warm showers. There were taxis on the tarmac streets and the restaurants had plate glass windows. It felt luxurious and civilised although this was one of the most isolated towns we would visit on the trip. Ali's road links with Western China mean that it is populated by a significant proportion of Uighurs, a Muslim race of Western China, similar to the Central Asian races. In the restaurant the young boy who served us wore a white skullcap and his mother a headscarf. Their faces were heavier and noticeably more Caucasian than the Oriental and Mongol features we had become used to. The food was different too. We ate big chunks of lamb on skewers with chilli paste, and, instead of the soupy butter tea of the Tibetans or the jasmine or green tea of the Chinese, we drank the coppery red tea of the Uighurs.

Now we had made it to Ali, we were faced with the prospect of persuading Norgay and Sonawangde to let us leave them and make our own way west to Kashgar. We had kept quiet about this plan, only discussing it when Norgay and Sonawangde were not around, as we were worried if they knew we planned to head west they would refuse to take us as far as Ali. We had even considered not telling them at all, just disappearing in the night, leaving a note telling them we had gone; but in the end we had got to know them too well to deceive them and we also doubted our chances of success without their advice.

The trip from Ali to Kashgar involves crossing the Aksai Chin, a triangular shaped territory at the edge of the Tibetan plateau. Both China and India lay claim to this piece of land, which is why access for foreigners is so sensitive, with the threat of fines or deportations for those attempting to travel on it. However, the allure of these isolated and forbidden territories was strong. It was an unrivalled emptiness, with nothing more than a single-track road marked on the map. The depressing alternative was to retrace our steps back to Lhasa then make a ten day bus trip around Tibet through the southern Taklamakan desert, where the Chinese mined asbestos and, so the rumours went, tested their nuclear weapons.

While we were eating that evening, we broached the subject of our planned departure. It was a tense moment but neither of them seemed surprised by our plans; maybe they had already worked out what we wanted to do from our insistence on visiting Ali. Norgay smiled and shrugged; a drive back with no foreigners presented no problems, they would just throw away the permits and pretend to be independent Tibetan travellers. As long as we could find transport, they were happy to let us go, and told us plenty of trucks went west every day. Sonawangde was shaking his head.

"You must think us mad," I asked him, "giving up the comfortable jeep for the back of a truck?"

"No," Sonawangde replied, "I have been a driver for twenty-six years and I know what it is like to want to see places. I am just sad you will not be with us on the journey back to Lhasa." He was still smiling.

CHAPTER 6

Aksai Chin

I didn't sleep easy that night. My mind raced through scenarios, few of which ended in Kashgar. Would a driver take us? What would we do at the checkpoints? Would Norgay get cold feet and change his mind? Would we (and here was the alternative) have to get back into our jeep and go back to Lhasa then around Tibet, another two weeks on these roads. There was more to it - I didn't acknowledge it at the time but driving on this road was about more than just the time saved. The very illegality had become a reason to do it, a proof of something.

We got up at eight and gave Norgay and Sonawangde our remaining food, a spare rucksack, cigarettes and letters excusing them from any responsibility for what we were about to do. We agreed that we would meet in the same restaurant if we were turned back within the next 24 hours.

"I think you will get through," Sonawangde told us, "there are many trucks going to Kashgar."

"See you tomorrow," said Norgay, rather less optimistically.

Simon guarded the luggage in the truck depot teahouse while Julia and I went to try to get us a lift. We decided this was the best strategy as Simon's hair and beard were now sun bleached, while Julia was half-Chinese and I was at least dark (if a conspicuous foot taller than everyone else in the town.)

Our bags were disguised in China Petroleum plastic-fabric bags, and we wore our fur collared PLA olive jackets. For all our trouble I don't actually believe we fooled anyone.

The truck stop was on a three-way junction, and at eight in the morning, it was just waking up. On the back of the trucks were layers of blankets piled over immobile sleeping drivers. Loads of timber and building materials lay in heaps on the central island, waiting for onward transport to the East. From time to time engines roared into life then spluttered to death again as the mechanic reached into the black machinery between the open jaws of cab and wheel base.

It was too early; no one was leaving yet so we retreated to the teahouse, for bowls of red tea. The tea house owner pulled a hobbled sheep towards a shallow brown dish one table away from us. He knocked the sheep onto its back with his knee and pulled back the head of the animal, his knee dug into its belly holding it immobile. He placed the dish under the sheep's head and drew his knife across its straining neck, with three quick silent strokes, catching the steaming blood, which spewed from the cut in the dish. He continued holding the head, jaws clamped together, as the legs kicked and the severed windpipe rasped as if the lungs were trying to catch one last breath from the open neck. Its eyes flickered and rolled. In thirty seconds it was motionless.

It was a vivid demonstration that we were on the edge of Buddhist territory and from now on meat not barley flour would be the staple. We ate fresh kebabs from the rapidly butchered sheep, washed down with more red tea. The chunks of meat, with a smoky aroma from the open-air barbecue, were too delicious for us to be squeamish about.

The first driver looked at us nervously and pretended not to understand. Finally, he told us he was not going to Kashgar, and slammed his door. Two or three other drivers had similar reactions, "not leaving today…no room…already have passengers…" Then we met Yessin. He was getting up even later than the other drivers, his curly hair tousled and sticking up from the side of his head where he had been sleeping. His eyes were still half closed, but he considered our request and nodded nonchalantly. Two hundred yuan, no bargaining, and he was only going as far as Yecheng (it didn't matter; that was only a few hours by bus from Kashgar).

"Wait in the cab while I eat my breakfast," he told us and wandered towards the teashop. We were nervous about this; we had already seen uniformed police and army vehicles patrolling the truck stop, and we had no individual permits for Ali, let alone for the road to Kashgar. We sat quietly in his cab, trying to look casual, sipping tea from our bottles. Half an hour later a PSB officer in full camouflage who had been wandering among the trucks noticed us and banged on the door of the cab with the flat of his hand, shouting something unintelligible. .

After all that hoping, it would be the long road for us. The easiness of it all had been deceptive. We ignored the officer; the door was locked. He turned to the small group who had come to see "the Americans," (as he described us) and talked to them earnestly. Then he walked away while the small group stayed watching us. We decided it would be safer for us not to be in the cab when the Tourist Police arrived, so as soon as the wide-eyed group had lost interest Julia hid behind the seats, while Simon and I moved to the open truck bed and pulled our luggage around us.

I heard the sound of someone clambering up on the wheel to look into the back of the truck.

This is it, I thought.

"You will be very cold in here. You should sit with us in the cab." It was Yessin. There was another painful five-minute wait while the mechanic bought tobacco then the engine revved, a deep guttural roar, a complaint from the arthritic gears and we were moving, past the lines of other trucks and out of the junction, towards the west. The PSB officer had not returned, I couldn't understand it, but I allowed myself to hope again. Maybe we would get away with it.

*

Yessin was a very experienced trucker. His three brothers were in the business, and, like him, made the journey from Yecheng to Tibet three times a month, during the six month period the road was clear of snow. They carried heavy goods from the oasis of Yecheng to Western Tibet. His mechanic sat wordlessly beside him, rolling him endless cigarettes from woody tobacco in little strips of newspaper. They were both Uighurs but we knew no Uighur so he spoke haltingly to Julia in Chinese, with hand actions where he did not know the words. "They have no trees, we take them wood. It is too cold for melons and tomatoes so we take them too." There was not much to bring back from desolate Western Tibet but sometimes they could pick up a load of freshly blasted stone from the road menders to supplement the £100 a month, which already was a good wage for a twenty year old. Taking us on the journey at his non-negotiable fare would net him over a month's wages and was certainly worth the risk of any fines.

It was September, and this would be the last run of the year. In Yecheng, Yessin would get married, a thought that made him grin at us – straight teeth slightly stained by tobacco, white straw hat pushed back on his head.

A few hundred metres out of Ali we saw a lonely figure, half-hiding behind one of the large boulders cleared from the road, a rucksack poorly concealed nearby. He was having some difficulty, as the rock was not quite large enough to hide his tall frame. It was a surprising sight in the empty landscape, and especially strange when we realised he was a Westerner. When he saw that our truck was alone, he came out from behind his rock and stuck out his thumb, in formal request. Yessin, stopped the truck and opened his window, but he could not understand a word of the hitchhiker's request. Julia was brought in to translate. She looked daggers at him – *this was our ride, and we didn't need another body in the cramped cab*, but Yessin enthusiastically nodded at the prospect of another fare. So we met Phillip.

He was a German photographer, who had made his way west by public bus to Kailash and Ali. That was already an admirable achievement. I had dismissed the possibility of travelling by bus as it was impossible to get permits without booking a jeep, and we had seen how many checkpoints there were on the road west. Somehow Phillip had managed it. He had been waiting for a lift to Kashgar for three days, and had been told he would be better hitching outside the town where truck drivers were less nervous about picking up passengers. He had not met with much success so far and had been left in a cloud of dust several times when linguistic difficulties had stifled his attempts at fare negotiations. Half of the traffic on this road was military and Phillip was understandably nervous about being noticed this far away from Lhasa (the only place he was officially allowed to visit.) This was why he had concealed himself, albeit rather inadequately, behind the boulder.

The seating arrangements were re-organised. The driver and the mechanic sat on either side of the cab, on the seats, with Julia in between them, sitting on the ledge that covered the gearbox. In the bed compartment behind the seats Philip, Simon and I squashed together, our knees in our faces and all our legs crossed together in a pile. Phillip could not have been a worse shape to share a confined space with. He was very tall and so thin from his travels that he looked like his whole body had been stretched length-wise. He was uncomfortably bony and we would be cramped in a tiny bed with his angular limbs for three days.

He had done a photo story on the Kailash pilgrims and now he was heading west where he wanted to do some shots of the Kazakh hill men who use eagles to hunt. When the photo stories were good he sold them to serious geographical or travel magazines and when they were less impressive the in-flight magazines snapped them up, funding a life of travel interspersed with deal-signing at his base in Hong Kong.

*

We reached the first army checkpoint after dark. Yessin had refused to let us attempt the walk around the checkpoint and now we saw why. On one side a lake stretched into the distance and on the other a crumbling cliff ran along the hills, which disappeared into the darkness. The checkpoint was buzzing with activity. Olive green uniforms scampered about haranguing the drivers in trucks in front of us. Further away there was a scuffle and six or seven soldiers landed punches and kicks on a Tibetan, half crouched his arms protecting his head. "He is a Tibetan, but he has no papers for this road," Yessin explained, his eyebrows lifted. Yessin knew we had no papers either. He looked as nervous as we did as we followed him wordlessly into the guardhouse.

It was lit with bare bulbs, faces looming out of the narrow doorways. Someone shouted at me to go outside with the other foreigners. We waited nervously for inspection. The soldier who took our passports didn't look much over 17. He was close to five foot and he barely filled his uniform, which hung from his shoulders in folds. A cigarette pointed downwards from his lips, gangster style, and every word came out in a gruff cloud of smoke.

"And your permits?" He demanded.

Julia bluffed, "Tibet Tourism Board told us we do not need permits"

"You must have permits."

"Oh, we are very sorry. But we came from Lhasa and understood there was no need for permits. We have to catch a flight from Kashgar in four days."

"Where to?"

"Turkey. All of us. In four days. We need to fly from Kashgar very soon."

The young soldier's eyes darted over each of us. He took two deep inhalations in quick succession and winced at us through the smoke. I could see him weighing us up; of course we were lying, foreigners weren't allowed to come this way at all but he had other things to deal with; Tibetans without papers were an easier target.

"Do not ride in such big trucks again." He turned to leave us.

"And you," he pointed to Yessin, "come with me." Inside the guardhouse he was fined for each foreigner he was carrying and a soldier was sent out to count us by shining a torch in each of our faces. Yessin added this fine to the amount we had agreed to pay him for the ride West. It wasn't going to eat into his profits.

*

At night we stayed in a truck stop, a desolate wind-scoured line of single-storey buildings with a bunkhouse and a line of trucks. There was an air of the Wild West Saloon when we entered the restaurant: two foreign men making a feeble effort at disguise in padded Chinese Army surplus jackets, one emaciated giant, and a woman travelling without husband who bedded down on the sleeping platform with the other men. The laissez faire attitude of Tibet had been quickly replaced by the strict Uighur moral line. Yessin enjoyed the attention and pointed out with glee that Julia was an American.

In the morning we were already driving as dawn came slowly over the hills, revealing iced-up streams, which cracked as we forded them. The truck lurched and bumped more than the jeeps but in the churned up wet areas the weight and long wheelbase of the truck were distinct benefits. It felt like being transported in a tank. I looked out the windscreen with eyes still gummy from sleep at our lonely road and rock formations like decaying teeth, looking not quite solid in the haze of dawn.

At one river we interrupted what looked like roe deer and Yessin, whooping, swerved off the road onto the flat plain, chasing the startled animals. They swerved and jigged like rabbits narrowly escaping our bonnet, while Yessin lifted his hand from the wheel and leant backwards like a cowboy on a bucking bronco. They scattered and we ploughed back to the road. Yessin looked round at our surprised faces, eyes half closed, tongue between his teeth chuckling. Diversions like these were necessary to relieve the boredom of this slow, unbending road.

The strain of this high altitude unsurfaced highway forced us to stop frequently to let the mechanic adjust the elaborate cardboard patchwork on the radiator grill that regulated the engine temperature. We rose above the snow line through starkly beautiful scenery. Mountains flowing with snow-covered glaciers piled on top of one another until they met the sky. Even the colour of the sky reflected the altitude, a light silvery blue as if there was not enough air to make it a deeper colour. Occasionally we came across shadowy lakes hemmed in by hills, with ice-scabbed sides, but mostly the panorama was an unvarying white, with the brown, muddy streak of the road down the centre. We left Tibet proper shortly after midday over a 5,200m pass, and started the two-day drive through the Aksai Chin.

*

In 1955 the Welsh climber, Sydney Wigall illegally entered Tibet to make an attempt on Gurla Mandhata (the mountain that we had seen towering over Lake Manosarwar.) But this was not a normal mountaineering expedition. Wigall had been recruited by Indian intelligence officials to spy on the Chinese whom they suspected of building a road to Western Tibet in preparation for a possible invasion of the Indian territory of Aksai Chin. However, his expedition was soon captured by the Chinese and imprisoned in Tibet, where they were subject to brutal interrogations for two months. For intelligence gathering purposes their captivity turned out to be a blessing as Wigall was able to discover from his captors that the Chinese were indeed building a military highway West and that they did have designs on parts of North India. Eventually Wigall's group was released and managed to make their way back to India in terrible winter conditions. However, when their discoveries were made known to Nehru (the President of India) he dismissed them, believing that the Chinese could not be so two-faced as to pursue a policy of friendship whilst planning an invasion of this small territory. But Wigall's information was correct, the Chinese had been building a road across the Aksai Chin as early as 1955. It was not until 1959 that India finally sent patrols into the area, which were then attacked by the Chinese forces guarding their newly built strategic highway. The Chinese claimed they needed the road for access to Western Tibet but no compromise was to be reached with India and on October 20 1962 the conflict erupted into open war. The road we were now driving along was the spark of this bitter dispute. [9]

It was a short-lived series of battles, a cease-fire being declared just over a month later. However, the fighting conditions must have been horrendous. We felt the cold already, but winter would have arrived in earnest by October and contemporary photographs show soldiers trussed up in greatcoats, leaning behind walls to shelter from the wind. The Indian wounded froze to death in the night as they had not been equipped with tents, sleeping bags, or warm clothing. Official reports show around 500 deaths on either side, but behind the statistics are terrible stories. One particularly striking account was of the C Company of the 13 Indian Army Kumaon Regiment who were defending the tiny village of Rezang La three days before the cease-fire was announced. Of 127 men only 14 survived, of whom 9 were severely injured.

[9] "Spy on the Roof the World," Sydney Wigall, Canongate 1996.

Maybe it was a battle better left forgotten as their corpses were not discovered until January 1963, when a shepherd reported seeing numerous bodies frozen solid where they had died, covered in a light shroud of snow.

Nowadays, the road is under Chinese control but it is only used for the limited commerce between Eastern Tibet and Xinjiang. The area remains frighteningly isolated and I wondered at the numbers of bloody deaths for these kilometres of emptiness and a muddy road.

*

All afternoon we trailed across this desolate land and saw only two buildings; crude shacks made from plywood and striped polythene, which served bowls of thukpa. Outside, a patch of bloody ground where lunch was slaughtered, the blood draining from the body into an iced up puddle. In one of the restaurant shacks I saw the goat's severed head looking up at me from under the bench as I slurped my lunch, its tongue lolling from one side of its mouth like a cartoon depiction of death. Behind the shed was another trussed up animal waiting for its turn the next day.

The climb to the high passes was a painful grind even in the lowest gear. Yessin leant over his wheel and urged the truck towards the next hairpin bend with furrowed brows. The air was thin at this height and the engine whined from lack of oxygen. I wondered how they ever got over the passes when carrying a full load. We paused at the top and allowed the sharp wind to blow into the radiator, then coasted down, Yessin twirling the wheel in his arms sending the cab swooping over the edge of the road where a hundred foot drop waited. At particularly bad moments, Julia, sitting in the front seat gasped and Yessin gave his amused look to the lads in the back, tongue between his teeth, his eyes laughing. Further down, the road was covered in piles of gravel and sand, lying at regular intervals ready to be smoothed for re-surfacing. Avoiding these brought us even closer to the edge, but there was a confidence in Yessin's actions and it may have been this, or sitting too far back in the cab to see the drop which helped me to relax.

Soon the passes were behind us and, as night closed in, we made good progress along the banks of a swirling brown river. With the drop in height the air became warm and dusty. We stopped at a noodle house where a tiny television crackled in the corner. On the stove a group of enamel mugs bubbled and steamed, each one an individual noodle broth, their metal lids rattling against the rim as the steam escaped. They served us fresh orange melon, red peppers with noodles and cardamom flavoured tea. We could taste that we had left the desolate Aksai Chin and were now in Xinjiang province of China, getting closer to the oasis of Kashgar.

It had been dark for some hours and the road surface had stretches where it seemed to be getting better. Each time it improved I imagined it was the final stretch to Yecheng, then it would deteriorate again and we would be crawling over riverbeds that had reclaimed the road.

We came upon our final checkpoint suddenly, a bright light and a roadblock. We had expected more during the trip, but the road would soon be closed and the high altitude checkpoints had already been shut up for the winter. A young soldier stood alone beside the light and was visibly taken aback when four Westerners and two Uighurs loomed out of the darkness. He nervously flicked through our passports giving each a cursory glance and a nod. Yessin had told us to claim we had not come from Tibet, but to tell some convoluted story about a broken-down jeep on a Xinjiang tour; we were now out of forbidden terriroty. In the event we were waved through after a cursory inspection and not even asked our route.

There was still a long way to drive in the dark but a feeling of relief flooded through me, nothing could turn us back now. It seemed the uncertainty of the last few days was over. We were not prepared for the violence of the final hours of our journey.

*

We were driving through a small town, which spread for 50 metres on either side of the road. In the middle of the stretch of houses stood a stationary truck, with a group of people gesticulating at one another in the glare of its headlights. We braked with a lurch that sent us tumbling together in the back. Yessin and the mechanic jumped out of the cab and joined in the shouting. Quickly the argument turned violent and punches and kicks were thrown, still dramatically lit by the headlights. The group from the other lorry grabbed concrete re-enforcing poles from the back of their truck and were swinging the wobbling lengths around their heads as they stood on the bed of their truck. My position in the open door of the truck suddenly felt more precarious. I ducked in just as I saw our mechanic take a blow to the back of the legs with a long handled shovel. He buckled slightly but remained standing.

The four of us cowered in the cab, not knowing what to do. We had no idea what the argument was about or why our drivers were involved. We had little time to consider this as in a matter of minutes the group from the other truck roared off, knocking into our truck on the broadside and twisting the row of hooks used to tie on the canvas. The mechanic appeared out of the darkness, his face covered in blood and patches of red all over his golfing jacket.

He had a large split swelling under his left eye, which had thrown blood onto his forehead, and in dribbles down his face. We sat him on a charpoy at the side of the road and Simon held a torch in his face while I cleared away the dried blood from his cheek and moustache before mopping gently under his eye, holding the back of his head firmly as I imagined I should.

"Ah, doctor," a local who had appeared from the darkness remarked with satisfaction. He could not have been further from the truth. I felt nauseous confronted with the open pink of his cheek, and even worse was the smell of the mechanic's breath. He was still panting and it smelt of the Uighur tobacco he continually smoked and another smell of something stale and animal, a combination of 3 unwashed days in a truck cab and adrenaline.

While we were occupied with cleaning up the mechanic, Yessin had roared off in pursuit of the other truck leaving the four of us and the mechanic in the village. I had no shoes on, and on top just a thin cotton shirt. It was 3 am and very cold. But worse, my diary and camera were still on the truck, currently en route to another fight, and who knows what they did with the trucks of aggressors in these situations. We waited for an hour and the mechanic explained to us in his broken Chinese what it was about, the gauze on his face occasionally illuminated in red as he drew on one cigarette after another.

The other truck was run by Han Chinese, whom the Uighurs see as intruders in their part of China. The fight we had just witnessed was the result of steadily growing ethnic tensions. Xinjiang was annexed by China in 1759 but there is a continuing feeling of oppression among many Uighurs and an ongoing separatist movement occasionally erupts into riots or bombings.[10] But there was also low level violence between working men over stolen opportunities, perceived or real. China's long term strategy against Uighur separatism is to back up its political control of Xinjiang with ethnic measures, providing housing and job incentives to encourage Han Chinese to move to the region and dilute the ethnicity of the territory (the same process is at work in Tibet). In 1950 there were 200,000 Han Chinese in all Xinjiang. There are now 6 million Han Chinese and Uighurs make up less than 50% of the population. The financial incentives on offer to settlers have allowed them to undercut the Uighurs and take business from them, and this has increased the inter-ethnic bitterness.

Han Chinese who had settled in the West now dominated the truck routes that had been the preserve of the locals, the mechanic told us bitterly. "They have better trucks, they are the favourites of the government for new contracts. They are pushing us out and making us poor." What we had seen when we pulled into the town was a heated but peaceful argument between Han Chinese drivers and the locals who had refused to sell them food. It was too late they said, although the real

---

[10] Official figures claim Uighur separatists were responsible for 200 attacks between 1990 and 2001, causing 162 deaths and injuring more than 440 people. In the largest incident in 1997, around 100 people are reported to have been killed during a pro-independence uprising in the town of Ili. Since September 11, the Chinese have focussed even more attention on the Uighur separatists who, they claim, have links to Al Quaida. The US encouraged such beliefs when in January 2002 it added the East Turkestan Islamic Movement (ETIM) to its list of terrorist organisations.

reason was the unwritten rule that Han Chinese drivers eat at Han Chinese restaurants in Han villages and Uighurs likewise. The locals had retreated in the fight leaving Yessin and the mechanic to take on several Chinese truckers.

"That was always the way, the locals do not want trouble," the mechanic said. Yessin and the mechanic were like do-good cowboys, running the roads, righting the wrongs perpetrated by intruders and defending their livelihood. However, I knew things were never that simple. The Han Chinese were settled in Tibet and Xinjiang by the central government, they were not independent intruders. Had we not arrived when we did, then the argument would probably have dispersed without violence. The villagers seemed able to keep out of the fight and they were not being attacked when Yessin and the mechanic arrived. None of *them* was bleeding.

Our truck turned up an hour later. Yessin had not managed to catch up with the Han Chinese and he looked worn out, with dried blood in both nostrils. I felt ashamed for worrying about my camera.

At that moment the harshness of the road seemed very powerful. Building it over five years, against the landslides on the steep passes and the ravages of six-month winters, going to war over the territory it ran through, wiping out over one thousand men in a month, and now working the road continued to be a dangerous and violent trial. Crossing it illegally suddenly seemed less heroic.

*

Yecheng was still two hours away and there was nothing to do but carry on driving. The mechanic fell asleep, and Yessin stared into the darkness, breathing through his mouth. His eyelids drooped and sometimes closed completely. I passed him drinks of water and tried to keep him awake with inane questions,

"Is that Yecheng? How far to Yecheng? How big is Yecheng? How long until your wedding?" He didn't try to understand my sign language anymore and his eyes no longer laughed.

CHAPTER 7

To Kashgar

After 1100 kilometres of jarring roads cramped in a truck bed with unwashed companions, Kashgar felt like an Oriental pleasure garden. We lodged in the Chini Bagh hostel, luxuriating in real beds, warm showers, and a small tin of powdered Nescafe that we had found in the bazaar. It tasted amazing after so many weeks without coffee. We shampooed out the dust that had turned our hair stiff like incipient dreadlocks and at last we found a loo that we could sit and rest on, and read on. A fountain lit with red and white underwater bulbs erupted at dusk, and at the entrance, a uniformed gatekeeper saluted our taxi. The Chini Bagh hostel was formerly the British Consulate, and it was here that Peter Fleming had stayed after his gruelling five and a half month journey across China[11] over sixty years before.

"One night we slept on the floor, drank tea in mugs, ate doughy bread, argued with officials, were stared at, dreaded the next day's heat; twenty-four hours later we were sitting in comfortable arm-chairs with long drinks and illustrated papers and a gramophone playing, all cares and privations banished. It was a heavenly experience…we idled shamelessly in Kashgar, eating and sleeping and playing games…" Fleming goes on to describe the Russian Consulate, half a mile away. "Kini and I used to go there a good deal, to bathe in their

---

[11] "The News from Tartary," Peter Fleming. Jonathan Cape, 1936.

swimming-pool. They were always charming to us, but appeared to find us disconcerting."

Kashgar had been at the centre of the Great Game, when Britain and Russia vied for influence in Central Asia. These consulates were where paranoid and ambitious power games were played out. The diplomats in Kashgar became adept at the artificial two-faced relationship they had with their counterparts at the other consulate. A façade of cocktails and dinners thinly concealed their attempts at international espionage.

Fleming recounts one particularly entertaining aspect of this artificial relationship. The British knew that the Russian consulate had a wireless transmitting set kept illegally (they had no licence for it from the central Chinese authorities.) Out of politeness Fleming could not explicitly acknowledge the existence of the wireless to the Russians but he could ask them for news because their newspapers arrived from Moscow more quickly than the British news, that had to be brought by horse from India. "it was pathetic to see their faces cloud with concentration," he remembers, "their fingers unconsciously counting back the days, while they sorted out all that they had heard recently on the wireless from what would have been their latest news in papers a fortnight old."

Now both consulates had been decommissioned and turned into hostels. The former Russian Consulate was now called the "Seman Hostel". In the heat and stickiness of Kashgar's afternoons nothing would have been more pleasant than a cooling swim, but despite a number of searches and requests we could never find the Russian swimming pool that Fleming had bathed in. We decided it must have been filled in to allow space for another block of sprawling hostel buildings.

All of Kashgar had been subject to drastic rebuilding. Multi-storey Chinese edifices stared with dark windows over the institutional pastel tiling of municipal squares. New multi-lane highways carved through the edges of the mud brick old town. One house had been half knocked down where it got in the way of the road, leaving the debris of a half-demolished bathroom open to the road. The ancient mud brick city-wall had suffered a similar fate, bulldozed abruptly to let a four lane highway through leaving crumbling edges on either side of the road.

In the heart of the city, away from the new roads and tiling, the alleyways of the old town remained unchanged. The streets were narrow and overshadowed by storey upon storey of mud brick houses. No longer the squat, solid Tibetan houses, or the modern Chinese monstrosities; here the architecture had a distinct Islamic appearance. The mosques were a blaze of arches covered with plaster tracery that opened onto cool leafy interior gardens. The house gables were covered with baubles and crescent moons, and filigree windows in wooden doors gave onto courtyards where tiny fountains bubbled.

At the centre of the old city, was the Idkah Mosque overlooking the bustle of the central square. Streets ran away from the square like the legs of a spider, each one flavoured by the particular trade which took place there. On the metalworkers' street was a constant clatter as pots, stoves, shovels and trunks were hammered out of sheet metal and a higher-pitched scraping sound as apprentices etched arabesque designs onto decorative kettles with miniature chisels. In the woodworkers' street we waded through the curls from the lathe and sneezed on airborne sawdust. The dentists' street was quiet as though people were afraid to walk along it. Open jaws grinned from garish, grisly diagrams in the windows and inside chairs were tilted at the ready or ominously curtained from view. The milliners sat cross-legged in front of their sewing machines with a wall of hats behind them, facing one another from their hutch-like shops the length of the street. In the middle of a wider street, fruit and vegetables were heaped in overflowing piles, shielded from the sun with broad umbrellas. At night, the main square filled with a vast array of food stalls, each lit with a single bare light-bulb: deep fried fish, chicken legs, whole poussins, noodles, sweet pastries and line upon line of kebab sellers. Some stalls looked more appetising than others, and I was not taken by the boiled goats' heads, but for the sake of Simon's portfolio I bought one and nibbled gingerly at what looked like the most innocuous bit of meat, which turned out to be the gum. It was a strange sensation to scrape your teeth against those of a goat, while chewing its rubbery gum. We left the head uneaten and filled up on the staple Uighur dish of plauv (rice with mutton), scooped up with rounds of sesame-covered bread, finishing up with a slice of sweet, cantaloupe melon.

As an important trading hub lying on the edge of China and bordering the Indian subcontinent and Central Asia, Kashgar has always been a melting pot of cultures and ethnicity. Sven Hedin, who passed through Kashgar on his way to Kailash, commented on this rich mixture.

"In Kashgar one finds a practically inexhaustible variety of types belonging to the most widely different peoples and with roots in all the countries of Central Asia. Indeed, even China proper, India, Persia and West Turkestan have through trading and intercourse and caravan connections contributed to the Babylonian confusion and blending prevailing in this the world's most continually situated city, from which at all points of the compass the distance to the sea is unthinkably great."[12]

The range of hats being worn in the market colourfully illustrated this ethnic variety. The younger Uighurs wore stiff four-cornered hats made from green and white embroidered material while the older men from the country wore amazing tall black velvet hats with fur lining and trim. The Mao cap was also popular among the Uighurs, designed like the old British flat cap, in dark blue, black, or sometimes checked tweed for the dandies. The Kyrgyz wore high white felt hats like elongated pyramids with black trim and stitching. The Uzbek hat was similar in design to the stiff Uighur four-cornered skullcap but made of black material with a white embroidered pattern. The Pakistanis either wore flat Chitral wool hats with a rolled brim or plain white cylindrical skullcaps. Apart from the Chinese, very few men went without a hat, and even young boys sported grubby caps with frayed edges and dented corners.

Phillip and Simon wandered the markets together swopping photographic tips. Julia and I wandered Kashgar too and got drawn into conversations with stallholders, hawkers and the tea-drinking idle. But all of us now needed time to recuperate and the days were short, beginning after brunch and ending early in the afternoon with coffees on the Chini Bagh terraces.

*

Our favourite eatery was the "Pakistani café," directly opposite our hotel, where delicious pumpkin and spinach curries were served with piles of fresh steaming chapattis. The café mainly

---

[12] "Sven Hedin Life and Letters," Sven Hedin, 1964.

catered for Pakistanis who traded goods back and forth along the Karakorum Highway, which runs between Kashgar and Islamabad. They would eye us suspiciously to begin with but end up talking animatedly about world politics, the war that had happened and the wars that would happen.

One group we always seemed to meet up with (mainly because they stayed next door to us at the Chini Bagh and took all their meals in the Pakistani café) was a group we called the Pakistani Playboys. There were three of them, but unlike the other Pakistanis they were not traders. They were on holiday. "We come to Kashgar because the girls and the drinks are cheaper here." They emerged from their room in the late morning and cracked open beers straight away. They reminded me of the Brits abroad on the Costa del Sol, milking as much hedonism as they could for a week, and sticking to their familiar national food. While football-shirted Brits might go to an ex-pat greasy spoon and fight off a hangover with egg, chips and brown sauce, the Pakistani playboys knew there would be aloo gobi and chana dal in the Pakistani café - food they could trust. They were all from rich families in Islamabad, and there was the hint that they had been sent away for the month of the Pakistani elections in case there was trouble (which suggested their fathers were in high places.)

Hvar, at twenty-five, was the oldest, and always took the lead in conversations, speaking with authority on every subject. He had played cricket for his province and his father was the chief of Police in Lahore. Ali was the youngest and had a rubbery face creased from smiling. When Hvar talked too much about politics, he whistled and looked at the sky, not dominant enough to interrupt, but showing us that he was bored by such serious talk. The third playboy was Imran, the Romeo of the group, with long gelled hair that he flicked from his eyes and matching tight jeans and denim jacket. While the other two talked to us, Imran made eyes at the shy daughter of the Pakistani café owner.

In the evenings we would sit on the terraces that ran around the open-air courtyard of the hotel and drink Xintaong beer, while they told us stories.

*

Despite the huge letters on the giant bazaar warehouse, which read "KASHGAR SUNDAY BAZAAR," it was in fact open every day. We had dropped in on a Thursday, and wandered around the stalls trying on hats and munching on fresh kebabs in the surrounding teahouses. It was a different undertaking altogether on a Sunday. The few melon sellers, surrounded by their stock had expanded to create a half-mile long pile of melons. The quiet hat store owners were transformed into near hysterical barrow boys, the carpet sellers tugged our sleeves and didn't let go, and there were no seats in the surrounding teahouses. Sunday is make-or-break day, when 50,000 people from the surrounding countryside and from surrounding countries descend on Kashgar to trade at the huge market.

The animal market had recently been moved a ten minute drive away from the central Sunday bazaar to prevent the unhygienic and disruptive arrival of herds to residential Kashgar every Sunday. A haze of dust, raised by the hundreds of trampling hooves, hung in the air over a sea of skullcaps perched on top of shaved heads. Lines of sheep were tied together at their necks creating a tidy herringbone effect while nearby freshly cut sheep carcasses hung from hooks, their mountainous fatty buttocks blue veined and shiny white in the sun. Just as we have bred sheep to have thick coats of wool in the west, the Central Asians have bred their sheep to have huge reserves of fat on their buttocks. The momentum of their swaying behinds gives the larger sheep an absurd wobbling walk but supplies the Uighurs with the ingredients for the perfect Kebab, with the ratio of one chunk of meat to two chunks of fat all the way down the skewer. Past the sheep were metal rails where cows and camels were tied up and finally the busiest area of all, the donkey market. Donkeys are now not allowed as a means of transport on the main streets of Kashgar, but they are still essential in rural areas to pull carts or carry spades, mattocks, and crops back from the fields.

I watched the negotiations for the sale of one donkey. An old white-bearded man, wearing a skullcap with yellow embroidery stood clutching Y450 (about £38) and eyeing up a small grey donkey. The donkey's back only reached the height of my stomach and moisture from its eyes had dribbled down its cheek giving the tiny animal a pitiful expression. The old man whose eyes were scarcely visible from the wrinkles on his cheeks was shaking hands with the owner over the donkey's back. A constant hand shaking takes place during the whole negotiation process and does not necessarily signal the sealing of a transaction. Something was wrong with the offer and the owner would not accept the old man's money, he let go of his hand and turned him away. The old man protested but the seller was not interested he was trying to attract another buyer. I carried on standing near the donkey and saw the old man look back mournfully one last time at the small donkey that he could not afford.

No one tried to sell me anything in the animal market.

*

I was immediately struck by how well developed the Apak Hoja tomb site was. There were several souvenir shops, a cultural museum and two ticket offices which issued ingenious tickets that doubled up as pre-paid postcards. I was surprised how popular it was with Chinese tourists; two separate bus loads of Chinese tourists rolled up as I did, the men festooned with massive cameras, their shirts rolled up to reveal their bellies (the curious national habit of the Chinese man in the heat.) I had not seen so many Chinese tourists since Lhasa. Elsewhere in Kashgar the emphasis was on Sinification in architecture and demography. Overtly Uighur monuments were relegated in importance; the Tomb of Sayyid Asla Khan was decrepit and unrestored and was being used as a public urinal; the ancient Uighur city walls were knocked through with roads. However, the Apak Hoja mausoleum with its neighbouring mosque and minaret shaped pillars at each corner, although equally Uighur in appearance, was being treated quite differently.

The reason for the special treatment of this site is because of one tomb in particular - that of the fragrant concubine. The fragrant concubine was a Uighur maiden in the harem of Emperor Qianlong (1711-99), who was said to naturally emit a pleasant fragrance. Born in 1734 she was chosen to be an imperial consort at the age of 22. The facts of her life are heavily contested. She may have been captured, or gone willingly to court; she may have committed suicide rather than sleep with the emperor, or she may have risen to the top rank of the concubines and remained in that position until she was 55. The line that the Chinese authorities have taken is that the fragrant concubine was a devoted consort of the Emperor despite her background in Muslim Xinjiang and this makes her a symbol of the cohesiveness of the Chinese empire. Outside the mausoleum a large sign in Chinese, English, and Uighur read,

"Love between the Uighur maid and the Emperor is an evidence for great unity among different ethnic groups in China. This structure is ranked as a key cultural relic." It was *because* of rather than despite the characteristically Uighur design that this mausoleum was so important to the story of Imperial unity. My guidebook told me that somewhere in a nearby graveyard was the tomb of Yakub Beg, the leader of an independent Kashgaria that broke away from Chinese rule in 1865. But despite wandering around and asking at the cultural museum, I could not find it. The story of Yakub Beg has the opposite message from the authorised story of the fragrant concubine - division, disunity, and self-determination. On the tourist leaflet the fragrant concubine's grave was the only site indicated on this side of Kashgar - a large blue dot with the curve of the domed mausoleum. I was reminded, as one is from time to time, that history is more often about what is happening than what has happened.

In the peaceful gardens beside the mausoleum I noticed a photographer's team setting up a shot with a pretty Uighur model dressed up as the fragrant concubine. She had olive skin and long shining hair blowing free from a fallen headscarf. She pouted and posed among the waving yellow flowers of the courtyard garden. I imagine these images will grace next year's ticket, ready to be sent off across the People's Republic on prepaid postcards, reinforcing the story of imperial unity.

*

Our successful exit from Tibet across the Aksai Chin meant we had plenty of time to spend in Xinjiang before our visa to Kyrgyzstan began. Simon wanted to spend this time in Kashgar, the bustle of the market made for exciting photography but the Pakistanis in the café were particularly insistent we should explore along the Karakorum Highway, on the high altitude road towards their country. Our meetings with Pakistanis, like our meetings with the Indians at Manosarwar had exerted a strange pull on me. It made their countries seem less foreign and more inviting in contrast to the strange unknown of Kyrgyzstan and Iran. But our route was fixed and my trip down towards the Pakistani border was as far as I could go. We agreed to split up, I would follow their advice and go toward the border and meet Simon and Phillip back in the Chini Bagh Hotel a few days later. Julia had gone east to Hotan and we had made tentative plans to meet her there after I got back from the Karakorums.

The trip to Kashgar is an important trading opportunity for Pakistanis and the bus was delayed for four hours as their piles of luggage were crammed into every available space, sealing me in my seat. From halfway along the bus, the seats were completely buried under piles of blankets piled in see-through zip-up bags, so that the gaudy patterns made a sea of colour pressed against the windows. Boxes of grapes filled the aisle, two or three high so that when we stopped for tea I had to clamber along the arm rests to reach the door. One enterprising young trader had brought a consignment of second-hand portable stereos which lined the overhead compartments and slid around on top of the blankets behind me, shedding loose buttons, aerials and cassette doors.

Bus depot hawkers buzzed around as I waited for the loading, offering currency exchange, taxis and various fried snacks, sticky in plastic wrappings. The other passengers apologised for the delay but as the bus filled up they made last forays to a nearby market for more grapes and pears stuffed in straw (the central aisle had not quite been full.)

It was a cross-country bus, one of the thick-wheeled, high-slung models that plies the rough roads of Tibet and Western China. There was a lot of give in the suspension and on rough patches it felt like travelling on a four-wheeled trampoline. At each corner a ghetto-blaster swung round from the plastic covered blankets and delivered a solid blow to the back of my head. The windows were closed to keep out the dust and after a few hours the bus had the distinctive smell of the morning after a house party as the smoke of the "Gold Leaf" Pakistani cigarettes mixed with the rapidly fermenting juice that dribbled from the stacked boxes of grapes.

We passed out of the oasis of Kashgar, the trees stopping abruptly and giving way to the dust of the desert, before climbing into the foothills of the Karakorum. The road wound along the side of river valleys where water trickled in bleached channels. Next spring, with the fresh flow of melt-water the torrent would begin again and the car-sized boulders left balanced on their edges in the channel would start to roll, buffeted by a silty torrent. Above the road the cliffs were naked of vegetation and scored with ragged gullies ending in fans of scree. They leered over the vulnerable road, unstable and threatening.

It was almost winter and the road builders were beginning their work on the bridges in the brief period before the snow stopped work but while it was still cold enough to stem the flow of melt-water streams. Where a bridge was half finished a road diversion plunged away to a ford on one side. At a particularly steep diversion the river was almost vertically below us and the bus lurched clumsily towards the ravine on the crumbling side of the road. I clung to my seat with a sharp intake of breath, I knew we were top heavy with luggage piled high on the roof and that our trampoline suspension springs could easily detach us from the road. The brakes jammed on and we stopped with a great shuddering before accelerating on with a roar. The man opposite me twitched his moustache and chuckled, clapping his hands. "This road on Chinese side, very safe. Very safe. On Pakistan side, very steep. Many more dangers."

His attempts to calm my fears were not helped when we passed a group of three men wrapped in blankets against the cold, standing at the side of the road waving a red flag. The bus stopped and I clambered out with the rest of the passengers. The huddled figures pointed down the ravine with grim faces where, towards the bottom I could see a wheel and a few pieces of green twisted metal. Questions were muttered to the blanketed figures who pointed down and received small donations before we boarded the bus again. I asked the moustached man across the aisle what had happened. "It is a jeep which has crashed two days ago. Four people killed. These men are their brothers and the money is to help them - their wives and children."

It was an effective system. In this part of the world there is a macabre fascination with road accidents and spectators unashamedly gather at crashes. By exploiting this thirst for a spectacle, compensation was provided for the families of the uninsured casualties.

I couldn't live the life of these traders. I could only handle the Karakorum journey with the knowledge that this was something I would do very rarely, a one-off risk. "There and back, there and back," I reminded myself as I clutched the arm rests with greased palms and shook my head at the smoking, laughing Pakistanis who could drive this road without constantly watching the river beneath.

*

I woke with the dawn, put on my puffa jacket and hat and went out with my sketchbook. I had arrived in darkness the previous night, the Pakistanis shouting instructions to me as they roared off towards home. I managed to find the freezing cold "hotel yurt" on the banks of Karakol Lake and slept under a small hillock of piled blankets. I was now in the heart of the Karakorums, still in Xinjiang but close to the border with Pakistan. The sun was shining between the peaks of Mustagh Ata and Mount Konga which sit on the north and south ends of the turquoise lake. I breathed steam and gazed at the shadows changing on the sculpted ridges of the 7,000m peaks, the glaciers tumbling into dirty foothills, the faint ripples on the reflective water, and the wisps of smoke from the village to the south.

With the sun still low in the sky, I struck across the flood plain pastures where yaks grazed, and headed up the rocky valley towards the jailoo, the high pastures. A young Kyrgyz man in a dark blue Mao hat told me the jailoo was empty, the herds had been taken down for the winter, but pointed me in the right direction and told me to stay in Pangsa, his village, at the end of the lake when I returned in the evening.

The Kyrgyz communities around Karakol fled their homeland and settled in this part of mountainous West China at the beginning of the twentieth century. They came in two waves; first in 1916 when the Russians introduced conscription for the Great War, a move that spurred a general revolt in the Central Asian provinces and an outflow of people to escape both conscription and the bloodshed of the revolt. In 1930 there was another exodus as many Kyrgyz slaughtered their livestock and fled to China rather than submit to a policy of collectivisation dictated by Moscow.

Back in the shadow of the mountain it was cold again and I walked faster. Soon the scrubby grass of the lakeside petered out and the gradient increased. I cut out of the broad valley and kicked my way up the plaster of snow on the valley side. When I reached the sun again I stopped and ate one of the dumpling rolls I had saved from breakfast.

The ground rolled with false summits, the summit of Mustagh Ata emerging from above the scree, and disappearing again as the ground steepened. The slope became gentle and there was a fuzz of scraggy stems covering the rocky topsoil. I came across a circle of rocks lying around a blackened hearthstone and realised I had reached the jailoo. A short distance further on the pasture fell away and I was face to face with Mustagh-Ata. Like a submerged iceberg, I had only been seeing the top of the mountain from the lake. Now I could see the whole thing from the fields of moraine and crumbling glaciers at the base all the way up the dazzling white haunches to the summit where plumes of spindrift looked like streamers in the sky. An orange fox started a few metres from me, surprised at seeing anyone at this lonely abandoned place and danced away, with nervous glances across its shoulder until I lost sight of it far down the ridge.

I sat down with my sleeping mat propped up on a rock to shield me from the wind, and waited. The sun gave more glare than warmth but it was loosening the cornices high on the mountain and I watched as one tumbled down, sending up slow motion clouds of snow and several seconds later a deep padded rumble. Beyond the mountain the Karakorum Highway continued its way South, cutting through this massive landscape and meeting Pakistan at the Khunjerab Pass a few hours further on.

I descended a different way, zigzagging down steep ridges to where I could see yaks and camels congregating around a water pool. I had finished my water some time before, and the melt-water streams were all dry with the cold. But, when I reached the pool the yaks were being anti-social, standing in it, shitting and drinking at the same time. I would have to wait until the village.

It was mid afternoon by the time I got back to Pangsa, where the man in the Mao cap was stacking yak dung in piles to dry outside his house. His two sons looked at me curiously then hid behind their father's knees. We ate chapatti and aerean (watery yoghurt) and his wife began to make tea. I could smell the sharp scent of the leaves stewing on the wood burning stove. She added milk - even better - and stewed it some more, then poured me a bowl and offered me a plate of sugar (or at least it looked like sugar). I took a large spoonful and stirred it in, then took my first sip and realised it was salt. So thirsty and so looking forward to the tea, I regretted my mistake.

"Good?" the man asked, "good chai?"

It would be too rude to pour it away, "Yes, very good. Thank you."

I thought I had left salt tea behind in Tibet, though I later found it was popular across the Karakorums as a cheaper flavouring than sugar. He poured another cup but I had taken so much salt that it lay in a slurry at the bottom of my cup and tainted every re-fill I had.

His wife made dinner, chopping cabbage and stewing it with a tomato and chilli. The floor level stove had two openings, one near the chimney and one above the flames at the front. The holes were shaped so that the pot could be slotted completely into them. She boiled the cabbage on the hotter front hole then replaced the pot with a dome shaped chapatti griddle. Her rolling pin looked like a broom handle, and to roll large chapattis on her small chopping board, she let the dough wind around the wood in several layers, before dusting it with flour and rolling it up from the other direction. The dough hissed and bubbled on the griddle and in between twirling her broom handle she broke the air bubbles and flicked the chapattis over with a wooden paddle. We ate dinner seated round a plastic tablecloth, each scooping up the spicy cabbage with pieces of chapatti from the communal bowl. The two boys (aged two and four) fell asleep while we were still eating dinner and their father put them to bed under piles of blankets on the platform where we were sitting.

We had no common language and we sat around the stove in silence while the father smoked a cigarette. His wife laid out more blankets on the platform and I bedded down at one end, the taste of cabbage still in my mouth.

The boys started rolling around and giggling before dawn then got up and stumbled around the sleeping platform naked from the waist down. The whole family and I had all been lying in a row on the platform and the boys leapt over our prone bodies as if they were playing Chinese ladders. When their father shouted at them with weary early morning hoarseness, they giggled and jumped on him even more. At last he got up and stirred the ashes of the fire with an aluminium tube which he then used to blow at the sparks and light some flakes of yak dung. I went out in the early morning frost, and when I returned the wife had emerged from under the pile of blankets, her headscarf back on so that I was not sure if she had slept in it. Smoke filled the room as the flames snarled around the fibrous lumps of dung.

Breakfast was the previous night's chapattis broken into a bowl with salt tea on top (this time the salt was already in the tea – they must have assumed from my spoonful the previous day that I liked it). It was an effort to finish.

For another day I wandered among the camels and yaks on the common fields and circled the expanse of the lake. I watched it change from a hazy early morning light blue to a rich turquoise with the high sun at noon, and back to a translucent blue as the sun weakened between the peaks to the west. When I came to leave the next morning, the father wrote his address and told me I should return in summer 2003 when they would be staying in their yurt on the jailoo. I tried to pay him extra for his kindness but he would only take the small sum that we had agreed on for board and lodgings the day before. I looked at the written address, a swirl of old Turkic script with only the numbers written in Roman numerals, two-zero-zero-three. I walked back across the low common pastures with crunching steps in the frost. Behind me Mustagh Ata and Mount Konga shimmered in early morning haze as I waited for the bus to Kashgar.

CHAPTER 9

Taklamakan

For this part of our journey we had gone east from Kashgar to Hotan and met back up with Julia and Phillip (our companions from the hitchhike from Tibet.) This time we were not headed for a holy mountain but to an unholy waste - the Taklamakan Desert where lonely demons roamed. While mountains can be holy and the homes of the gods, deserts are held to be the home of devils and malignant spirits. I wanted to experience this natural antithesis to the holy mountain but to do this I would need to travel slowly across the desert like travellers had done in the past. I mentioned my interest in going into the desert to a Hotan carpet dealer. "You wanna ride camels, no problem, no problem. I get you camels. What about carpet? Made from camel's hair…." I took his words to be part of a sales patter, but the same dealer knocked on our hotel room door that evening and told us we could go into the Taklamakan for a four day trip by camel to the sand buried city of Rawak if we were available to leave the next morning.

The haunting devils of empty wastes are well known by those who live around deserts. The Turks have a saying that evil spirits play at ball in desert places while the Afghans believe that the solitudes of their deserts are inhabited by a lonely demon, which they call the Ghodlee Beaban (Spirit of the Wastes); a gigantic and frightful spectre, which devours travellers. They have also become a common experience of travellers in Central Asia. Having visited Tibet (see chapter 4), the Franciscan monk Orderic of Pordenone made his way west and described a terrifying experience while crossing a desert on his way back to Italy. This is possibly the most striking passage in the entire account and one that seems to convey such personal terror that it must be a genuine episode.

"I heard also therein sundry kinds of music, but chiefly nakers [kettle drums], which were marvellously played upon. And so great was the noise thereof that very great fear came upon me… And when I had gone in I saw there, as I have said, such numbers of corpses as no one without seeing it could deem credible. At one side of the valley, in the very rock, I beheld as it were the face of a man very great and terrible, so very terrible indeed that for my exceeding great fear my spirit seemed to die in me. Wherefore I made the sign of the cross and began continually to repeat Verbum caro factum… And so I came at length to the other end of the valley… But those who perished in that valley they say belonged to the devil."

Andre Migot enthused about the powerful spirituality of Emei Shan (see chapter 2) but was equally struck by the hellish sounds he heard in the desert. "They were like nothing I have ever heard before – groans, strangled shrieks, wails of agony… it seemed impossible to attribute them to any natural cause and my blood froze as I listened to them… It is still with me today, part of a whole gamut of strange experiences undergone in a land where things happen that happen nowhere else on earth." Marco Polo claimed: "Sometimes the spirits will call him by name; and thus shall a traveller oftimes be led astray so that he never finds his party… And sometimes you shall hear the sound of a variety of musical instruments, and still more commonly the sound of drums...." While the seventh century Chinese traveller Hsuan-tsang wrote specifically of the Taklamakan, "At times, sad and plaintive notes are heard and piteous cries, so that between the sights and sounds of the desert, men get confused and know not whither they go. Hence there are so many who perish on the journey. But it is all the work of demons and evil spirits."

Parts of the Taklamakan are the lowest land in the world, lying more than 100m below sea level. The temperatures across the desert are so severe that some rivers that run into the desert never reach the sea, but dry, wither and evaporate to death. The name Taklamakan means "Those who go in do not come out alive." It is no surprise that these scorching depths should be the home of maleficent devils.

*

The next morning we were standing on the fringes of the Taklamakan, an old Uighur man loading our rucksacks, jerry cans of water and finally us, onto a line of nine camels. They were raised with the guttural "Chucgk Chucgk" and a slap on their behind before they began their loping walk towards the dunes. The old man rode at the front sitting high on his camel to look for a route through the dunes. His white beard was so highly groomed that it looked like rigid plastic and stuck out at an unnatural angle from his chin, the full fist length required for a devout Muslim. He never removed his embroidered skullcap, but during the day he wore a broad-brimmed sun hat over the top of it. His assistant was half his age and not so picturesque. He carried a portable radio looped round his wrist all the time, tuning into stations broadcasting from Hotan, Kashgar and Pakistan; wailing Eastern songs that descended into fuzz and static the further we got into the dunes. His camel was piled high with blankets and mattresses and he lay on these with his radio dangling from his outstretched hand around the camel's knees. The leading camel was controlled with a rope attached to a peg in its nose, secured with a carved disc of wood at one end. With one hand the old man could pull the camel's head in the direction he wanted it to go and in the other he held a thin cane which he flicked at the camel's thigh to keep the speed of the caravan up.

These were Bactrian camels, smaller than the dromedaries of Africa with a good deal more hair around the head, neck, and stomach. The main difference was that these animals had two humps rather than one. The saddle was made of canvas stuffed with straw secured around the two humps with wooden poles. The movement on the saddle of the camel was more awkward than that of a horse, the gait longer and the roll of the back more pronounced. But once braced in position, slightly off centre so that it was the inner thigh rather than the groin pressed against the front hump, the lolloping motion of the beasts felt strangely dignified.

Things were less graceful when we had to descend steep dunes. On steeper sections the leading camel would speed up and those following would have their necks stretched out by the bridle so that they stumbled and tripped in the deep sand. The old guide would stop his camel at the bottom to look back at the train, creating a logjam as the animals tumbled into one another.

For two days our camels padded across the abrasive white dust of the Taklamakan dunescape. The scene had a dangerous beauty, an immaculate unblemished regular surface – a minimalist fantasy but a hostile place where nothing grew.

Sometimes Simon would jump down from the camel and wander away from the train to photograph us from a distance. The results were crisp and graphic – images that didn't look quite real. Silhouettes against dunes that looked airbrushed or computer generated in some way.

In the evening we climbed to the top of a dune above our camp and looked out over the dry sea that rolled and rolled to the horizon. We talked about the places we would go next, Julia would go back east to Hong Kong to see her son, Phillip to the Kazakh region to photograph hunting eagles, Simon and I to Kyrgyzstan. Then we talked about the places we would go to after that and after that until the world was criss-crossed with our trails and we felt like we would never stop moving. We talked until we were shivering because the sand bounced the cold of the desert back up at us just as it bounced the searing heat during the day.

*

Our second night in the desert, it was still dark, but nearby I could hear someone being sick. I poked my head out of my sleeping bag and looked around. A rivulet of sand ran into my eye from a crease in my sleeping bag. Through my watering eyes I could see Simon standing next to the dune, head bent between his legs, coughing. I wriggled out into the chilly night and took him his water bottle.

"Watch the shit," he mumbled. It had been a rough night for him. I made him some re-hydration fluid and dozed until dawn.

When the sun heated up for our second day we made the decision not to push on to the ancient city of Rawak. The old guide was complaining that the detour to the site would take far longer than the carpet dealer had originally suggested. In any case, Simon was feeling terrible, flopping backwards and forwards on his saddle with a shirt over his head to protect him from the sun. We made him a shelter from the blankets when we stopped for a long break at midday. Dehydration was a problem for all of us. The water was unpleasant, tainted by the plastic of the jerry can and chlorine purifiers and lukewarm from the sun. But as fast as we could drink it, we sweated it out and our sweat dried away as fast as our pores excreted it.

Air which had been stifling during the day became bitterly cold at night and we huddled around a fire made from dried roots dug from the desiccating sand and wore our warm clothes. The guide told us in broken Chinese his experience of the desert devils. He had worked with the camel trains all his life, but had only experienced the devils twice. He imitated the noise they made, a high moaning, followed by a confusion of crashes and hisses, which he demonstrated with much spittle. The assistant lolled around laughing at the stories but the old man's eyes were wide and stern. They stole camels from trains, snapping the halter ropes, and they accompanied the dust storms which blow over the desert lifting clouds of sand into the air, disorientating travellers and covering their tracks. I asked him what they looked like but he did not know. He had never seen one, only heard them and felt them in the darkness or the dust. He was an old man and did not revel in telling these stories. He told them in a matter of fact way, staring into the fire when he had finished, and answering our further questions slowly and with few words. After a bit he made his way to his bed roll, where he prayed. The assistant followed, his tinny radio hissing on as they slept.

WITH UNBLEST FEET

*

It was the unstable feeling in my own gut that woke me for the second time before dawn. I waddled across the cool sand to the other side of the dune, my stomach cramping as I crouched against the slope. We had been sharing plates and I must have caught whatever Simon had. Away from the campsite in the pre-dawn twilight the dunescape was featureless and untouched. As I crouched I imagined what would happen if I became suddenly disorientated, and forgot that the camp was round the corner of these dunes. If I walked the wrong way I would never know. Miles and miles of dune lay on every side, with no sign of which way was home.

Then I heard a sound, footfalls in the sand and a moan. Not a deep growling moan I had imagined a desert devil to make but a higher pitched adolescent cry, altogether more manic. My heart beat faster and I looked wide-eyed out into the shadows. It came again, a plaintive cry, and it was getting closer. I remained crouched, trousers round my ankles, immobile. Then I saw a baby camel emerge from the murk, bleating and lost. At night the camels were released from the train and hobbled to prevent them from straying too far. One of the young ones had become separated from its mother, and without being able to see the harmless source of the cries, they had sounded sinister. I had heard its cry all day as it chased after the train, but it sounded different in the darkness. Peering out into dunes, as empty as the sky, I understood how the imagination could work this into something far worse.

I walked back round the dune, relieved that the campsite was indeed still there. Phillip was pulling himself out of his sleeping bag, his face illuminated by the glow of a cigarette,

"You too?" he asked, "We are all coming down with it now."

*

The sound of drums mentioned specifically by Orderic and Marco Polo is a common theme in descriptions of desert hauntings. The British army officer and key player in the mid-nineteenth century Great Game, Alexander Burnes spoke of a sandy hill near Kabul that produced hollow sounds "very like those of a drum," while Sultan Babur, the Mughal leader, spoke of "the sounds of drums and nakers," in the desert. Desert travellers may have mistaken rock falls or sustained echoes from bare cliffs for devil's drums, especially when they were already disorientated by darkness. The other sound, mentioned by Hsuan-tsung and Migot, is of wailing and shrieking. The editor of Orderic's travels suggests that a possible explanation may be the sound of creaking sand. He cites the experience of Hugh Miller on the Hebridean Island of Eigg where the sand grains are particularly fine and footsteps make a squeaking sound like rubbing a freshly washed plate. I have visited the beaches of Eigg and remember the distinct creaks that each footstep made on the beach, known locally as the "singing sands." In dim light the squeaking of the multiple footfalls of a camel train could easily sound like shrieking demons.

Wild animals may also be a cause of these haunting desert noises. The German archaeological professor Albert von Le Coq described his experience at Bezeklik, a monastery complex in the Taklamakan, in his "Buried Treasures of Chinese Turkestan." "When all was still as death, ghastly noises suddenly resounded as though a hundred devils had been let loose." They rushed out to the terrace with their rifles to see what was causing these diabolical sounds. "There, to our horror, we saw the whole horse-shoe gorge filled with wolves that, heads in air, were baying at the moon with long drawn out howls." Von Le Coq goes on to describe how he and his companions shot one of the wolves and that after devouring its corpse the rest of the pack retreated from the valley.[13]

Despite the comfort of these explanations the eerie emptiness of the Taklamakan still played on the imagination. Here was a place where men did not linger. Travelling into the desert was a purgatorial journey, where survival was only on loan for a limited period, and it is small wonder that the desert came to be associated with a world of lost spirits. A world where geographical phenomena quickly seemed something supernatural and the sound of sand was terrifying.

*

We rode back to Hotan, through lunch, unwilling to sit out the midday sun in the desert and reached the trees on the outskirts by early afternoon. It had been a rather unsuccessful journey; we had not managed to reach the sand buried city of Rawak as planned, we had all got ill, and had as a result cut our time in the desert short. I had not seen the desert devils that had drawn me to the Taklamakan but I felt I had got close enough. I was glad to be leaving it.

On the fringes of the desert under the last of the trees, a family was picnicking on bread and watermelon and we sat with them in the shade, waiting for our taxi back to the

---

[13] "Buried Treasures of Chinese Turkestan," Albert von Le Coq, Allen and Unwin, 1928.

showers and fresh food of Hotan. Later, I would find a large camel tic in my armpit, which refused to detach even when smothered in Vaseline for twelve hours. We sat in the shade of the tamarisk trees and read Anna Karenina, Simon ripping out the pages and passing them to me as he finished them (we were down to our last book and were sharing it). Phillip complained that ripping up Tolstoy was barbaric, wincing and tutting every time a page was torn out.

Back in Hotan we said goodbye to Phillip and Julia. Phillip was already late for the eagle hunting season at the Kazakh border and caught the bus north. Julia headed back east, along the southern silk road to Hong Kong to her son and fiancée and where a new phase of her life was waiting, back in civilization but out of the ruthless world of commercial real estate.

*

Hotan's archaeological museum was set on the top floor of a dark block and the curator shadowed me as I wandered round, reading me the labels, despite the fact they were also in English. In pride of place at the centre of the hall were two mummified corpses, recovered from the tombs of the desert cities, toothily grinning up at me through their glass cases.

"There are few, few visitors here," he lamented, his eyes on the mummies so I wondered who he was actually speaking to. "Maybe when the road from Kashgar is improved there will be more. They are building an airport. Maybe this will bring more tourists."

A papier-mâché model showed sites dotted around the desert of Hotan along the line of the ancient silk route abandoned to the sands over half a millennium ago as new sea routes and religious tensions reduced overland trade between East and West to a trickle.

"Rawak, very good site. You have been?"

"No, unfortunately not, although we tried." Rawak was where we had been heading before stomach upsets and the desert forced us back.

"Very beautiful. Many things there, like coloured pottery, Buddhist buildings. But it is far away."

He pointed to a closer site, "Melikawat?"

"No, not yet. I would like to go."

"It is not so good as Rawak but - I will take you. Let us go, I have a friend with a car."

"What about your museum?" I asked.

"No road, no airport... no visitors." He shrugged and locked up the front door.

We drove past Hotan's temporary airport, a large rough surfaced field, with the diagonal line of the road across it, and continued between fields and the low walls of mud brick farmhouses. We walked the last kilometre along a road, deep in fine sand that sent up little puffs of dust with every step. A notice announced in Chinese characters and Uighur script that we had arrived at Melikawat. Far away on the left I could see the Hotan river and a few trucks waiting on its bank to take home the teams of jade hunters who scoured the river bed during the day, searching for the stones that washed down in the glacial melt water. A donkey cart came with a muffled clatter up the path behind us carrying a surly youth who sold me a ticket for the site.

I had guessed the curator to be Chinese, he was short with narrow eyes and fine cheekbones, but now he announced, "I am Uighur. Uighur good, Chinese bad." It was the characteristically fine bone structure of the Hotan Uighurs that had confused me, a bone structure that gives Hotanese women a reputation for great beauty. I asked him why the Chinese were bad and he related a convoluted, though familiar, story of job and house availability for Uighurs versus Han Chinese. "This is my country, why can they take, take…."

We were now walking near one of the few crumbling walls that remained standing in this lost city and the sand was covered with pottery shards. "Look, pattern." He announced, picking up a piece of pottery decorated with a regular floral pattern. "You keep it. Put it in your pocket. If you do not take it someone else will." It was an unexpected instruction from a museum curator, who I imagined should be concerned with the preservation of these Seventh Century sites. But the shards were so numerous that I couldn't help stepping on them so I did as he told me. For hundreds of metres all around us the sand was littered with pottery shards, mostly flat nondescript terracotta fragments, but the occasional piece with intricate decorations or the curl of a handle or spout.

"I was in Rawak last week," the curator continued, "and I found painted pottery. You are not allowed to take, but I take. The Chinese say you cannot take - they are worth maybe $20 or $50. But I am studying archaeology," he added in justification. "I have big box at home. Glass, jade, painted pottery. Very nice things. They are from my country, so I should have them. Chinese should not have them."

"You know Stein?" he continued.

"Yes, Aurel Stein," I answered, aware that he is extremely unpopular in China because of his large-scale removal of artefacts discovered in the Taklamakan sites in the 1900s. He shipped tonnes of books back to London found during his expeditions in the Taklamakan and even cut frescoes from the walls of cave temples before sending them back in sections packed in felt and straw.

"He take too," the curator noted with a smirk.

I asked if he disapproved of Stein's expeditions.

"No, no. The *Chinese* hate Stein. But I like Stein." He did not explain any further. But I understood from what he said earlier that someone who annoyed his enemy (the Chinese) gained his respect. There was also perhaps a sense of professional solidarity for another man who crossed the boundaries of archaeology into treasure hunting.

We wandered the huge site for a couple of hours as the sun dropped in the sky. The disconnected walls were isolated from one another, like the remains of a huge skeleton. They rose from the ground, badly eroded and looked like natural rock formations rather than buildings. Picking away at the base of one of them the curator found a minute green jade bead embedded in one of the mud bricks. He let out a low whistle as he picked it out between finger and thumb and held it up to the light, the tiny hole for the thread illuminated in the sun. I couldn't help feeling uncomfortable as I remembered the two inch thick text book - Renfrew & Bahn: Archaeology, Theories, Methods and Practice - which I had slaved over in my first year at university, with its emphasis on the highly scientific nature of modern archaeological techniques - cluster analysis - multi-dimensional scaling.

A boy arrived on a motorbike and the curator pointed at him. "He has found coins sometimes. He has very good eyes." Apparently the evening was the best time to look for coins, as the low angle of the sun glinted off any metal lying in the desert, which was gradually being harvested by these modern day treasure hunters.

CHAPTER 10

To Kyrgyzstan

I turned my head to gaze at the last I would see of the deserts of Xinjiang - not the rolling waves of the Taklamakan but an unattractive rock-strewn flatness. The desert met the mountains of the Pamirs, dry and crumbling on the Chinese side of the border. There was no greenery on the cliffs so I could see the sloping stripes of stratified rock - diagonal or vertical lines - that showed how the land had crumpled to make these hills. We stopped for lunch in a sad-looking village (which I could not find on my map) huddled round the army checkpoint for a suspension bridge across a dried up river. The wind gusted down the main street and left lines of grit on the boiled eggs we were eating for lunch. There was a definite sense of being on the edge of China. The village was populated by miserable-looking soldiers with not much to do and glum locals with not much to sell. Even the dogs were listless and bored, twitching half-heartedly while flies sought refuge from the wind in their coats and ears. Inside the restaurant, the soldiers' rifles were stacked in piles in the corner while they slurped noodle soup. They watched us, dull and silent, as we set off on the bus again, to leave their country.

There are two border crossings from China to Kyrgyzstan, the passes of Torugart and Irkeshtam. The guidebook told me that navigating the Torugart pass required a private jeep and a week's worth of form-filling and that the

Irkeshtam pass was only open to locals and commercial goods vehicles. Only once we arrived in Kashgar did we find out that after fifty years of restricted access, the Irkeshtam had at last been opened to foreigners in the past five months. There were two buses a week and we were told that we required no additional permits, only a one way bus-ticket, and a Kyrgyz visa.

It is likely that one of the last Westerners to use this pass before it was re-opened in 2002 was the mountaineer and British Consul to Kashgar, Eric Shipton, returning to war-time Britain in 1942. It was the quickest way to reach the railway at Andizhan (in current day Uzbekistan) and Shipton reported that "The whole journey took less than a month; half the time it had taken to reach Kashgar," from Delhi over the Karakorums with a train of ponies (the way he had arrived at Kashgar.) This was despite the fact that the faster route required him to detour in a large loop around Afghanistan; an illustration of just how isolated the Karakorum massif made Kashgar.

By mid afternoon we reached the dry red cliffs of the Irkeshtam pass and the new Chinese border post. The buildings were covered with light green and white tiles, and sparkled like a freshly polished bathroom. We waited while earnest guards searched our bus. At five in the afternoon the clock perched on top of a pastel green tower struck with an electronic synthesised version of the Big Ben chimes. It was ridiculous - a brand new musical bathroom set against the dust and rock of this desolate pass.

Inside, the customs officials were still learning how to use the computer and three of them crowded round when the time came to enter the details from our passports. The system could not cope with our data and after several minutes trying to enter our names on the flickering green screen, they resorted to writing them in an old logbook. Our bags were searched but customs were only interested in the paper and books we were carrying. My sketchbook was paid particular attention to, and the rather embarrassing photographs I had bought in Beijing of myself dressed as a Chinese Emperor and a Mongol warlord (sitting on a stuffed horse) were especially scrutinised, much to their (and Simon's) amusement.

There was half a mile of no-man's land hemmed in by razor wire before the Kyrgyz border post which featured long, single-storey wooden sheds with corrugated iron roofs, a contrast to the tiled extravagance on the Chinese side.

There were no computers at the Kyrgyz border post and we waited in a draughty bus shelter while the rest of the passengers looked increasingly fed up; everyone else was Chinese or Kyrgyz; it was our strange maroon passports which were causing the delay.

*

We crossed the watershed of the Pamirs. The land was suddenly lush and it seemed strange that we had driven through desert most of the day. Rivers fringed with bulrushes meandered across the flood plain between shadowy fields of pasture. The sun faded, casting long distorted shadows from the lines of cows trudging slowly with heavy, swinging udders. Behind them followed villagers with switches in their hands looking up at the bus with wider eyes and heavier noses than their Uighur neighbours. The style of the houses had changed too; the roofs were made of corrugated iron in a triangular shape. This served a practical purpose, leaving space for hay storage, but it was also a shape that suggested this was a place where it rained often. The farmland, the faces, the roof shapes and the climate felt familiar, as if in crossing the border we had made a huge step towards Europe.

The metalled road had stopped at the Chinese border post and it was rough and unsurfaced on this side. The bus suspension clattered as if protesting at leaving the easy, smooth road surfaces of China. I stretched out on my berth as the sun dipped behind gently rounded mountains and felt a surge of excitement at the prospect of a new country. I smiled to myself and glowed with self-satisfaction as the bus turned dark. All we had done was cross a border but I felt like I had done something original and clever. A year before I couldn't have placed Kyrgyzstan on a map, a dozen years before it didn't exist as a country and now we were driving across its roads, breathing its air. When I closed my eyes I imagined I could see the bus from outside, long headlight beams on an empty road superimposed on the map of Asia, like in a film, with the red line of our journey steadily heading west.

*

We woke to the unfamiliar sight of a cloud-covered sky. Osh is Kyrgyzstan's most ancient city but in the grey of our first morning it did not look an attractive place. The houses were plain concrete boxes, stained by dripping gutters. The official buildings had something of the industrial about them that fitted the soviet stereotype - a windowless post-office, a factory-like telephone exchange, ranks of identical apartment blocks.

Our room was on the top floor of the Allay Hotel by Osh's central market, the Jayma Bazaar. The bazaar is designed as a series of rambling concentric circles. The heart is occupied with food stalls, piles of apples, tomatoes, potatoes and leafy herbs, splashes of bright colour even in the subdued light. The outer circles are made up of hardware and clothes stalls, each one hooded with blue plastic against the pregnant clouds. The periphery of the market boasts no stalls, just old sheets laid flat on the ground. They are run by old women who sell pitiful displays of useless household objects; old telephones, doorbells, cutlery, and mildewed books (the old age pension is about £4 a month and this small amount goes often unpaid for months at a time.) In the street behind the Jayma Bazaar are the vodka shops. The Vodka is cheap (around 27p for ½ a litre), and most of the shops sell nothing else but three or four different brands of vodka, which sit at the front of the window, replacing the need for a sign. Most people bought it by the bottle, but it is also available by the shot to be consumed immediately. An old woman hunched unsteadily over her stick, reached up to a window and laid down two Som (three pence) for a shot that she drank in a gulp. She paused then laid down another two Som. It was a cold morning.

That evening, as we ate dinner, we experienced for the first time the aggressive hospitality of Kyrgyzstan where toasting is a competitive sport. Simon and I had ordered a bottle of vodka, which advertised itself as being "hangover free." We were celebrating our arrival in a new country and were already near our limits. The group at the table next to us, who had been drinking earnestly for some time before, joined us and ordered more bottles of the miracle vodka.

"Come, come, *friend*. What you say Cheer?"
"Cheers," we slurred.

There was no respite. The toasts followed one another with lethal rapidity and glasses were examined at the end of each toast to make sure no one was shirking.

"Cheeees. Cheeees. Come, come, friend. Karaoke…"

The night blurs in my mind shortly after that. I remember playing the only song on the karaoke machine with English prompts several times and I remember more of the bottles arriving and leaving. We moved off in a couple of taxis to a night club on the outskirts of Osh. We were sick of vodka so we drank sparkling wine from green bottles, warm and yeasty. The streets were empty when we left and we would have been lost were it not for the gleaming limestone spur of Sulemein which guided us back to central Osh.

I woke to a vice-like pressure on both my temples, that seemed to tighten every time I moved my eyes. My mouth was parched and sticky, with the sickly aroma of ethanol. Simon lay on the opposite bed, turned half onto his back. The claim of "hangover free" vodka, was not remotely accurate.

A shower would have been welcome that morning, even a cold shower, but for the second day running Osh was without water. Our toilet bowl was filling up and beginning to stink. We were told the water would be on at midday. But after an awful breakfast, where we hardly exchanged a word and where hunger and nausea followed one another in waves, there was still no water, and now the electricity had gone off. We sat in the dim hotel room with large bottles of water and felt sorry for ourselves. Not much was achieved all day; we were in no state to be clambering around our next holy mountain.

*

The weather was brighter and we were feeling a lot better (if not yet entirely well) after our day of purgatory. We met Anna as we walked past the foreign language faculty in Osh. She was impeccably turned out in a long black wool cardigan that hung to her knees over fawn velvet trousers. How she managed to look so fresh and keep her long hair so well groomed I have no idea, considering there was still no running water. We told her we had come to visit Mount Sulemein and immediately she insisted on taking us up.

"I'll be your guide. It is good for me to practise my English and you can hear the stories of the mountain. There are many stories…"

The craggy limestone and quartz peak of Sulemein sticks up from central Osh, giving relief from the lines of concrete housing blocks that dominate the skyline. Originally known as Bara-Kuh - Beautiful Mountain - it was renamed Mount Sulemein or the Throne of Sulemein at some point after the sixteenth century from a legend that the Prophet Sulemein had sat on the mountain to survey the city that he had founded. The rock that he sat on acquired an uncanny sheen which can still be seen today. The King and Prophet Sulemein of the Biblical Old Testament and Quoran (the son of David) was renowned as a traveller but there is no firm evidence that he ever came to this mountain or founded Osh. It is also said that the Prophet Mohammed once prayed at the mountain (this is even more unlikely than the legend about Sulemein) but because of the Prophet's rumoured visit the mountain is sometimes known locally as Kichik-Mecca (Little Mecca). It is now considered one of the holiest sites in Central Asia and it is claimed that climbing it three times is equivalent to making the pilgrimage to Mecca. The mountain is also said to possess curative powers for a range of ailments and Muslim visitors come from as far away as Turkey and Iran on pilgrimage to this holy mountain drawn by its legends and supernatural powers.

There was a concrete path all the way up to the "House of Babur," just below the highest peak of the mountain. Babur (1483-1530) was the founder of the great Indian Mughal State and an ancestor of the Emperor Shah Jehan who built the Taj Mahal in Agra. After being driven out of Samarkand in 1501 by the Uzbek Shaibanids, he looked for new land, first in Kabul and then in Northern India, where he took Delhi in 1525 and where his dynasty ruled until 1858. He was born in the nearby town of Andijan but grew to love Osh, and remembered it fondly in his memoirs.

"Orchards follow the river on either bank, the trees overhanging the water. Pretty violets grow in the gardens. Osh has running water. It is lovely there in the spring when the countless tulips and roses burst into blossom. In the Ferghana valley no town can match Osh for the fragrance and purity of the air." It was in Osh that the fourteen-year-old Babur chose to make his forty-day chilla (a period of silent meditation and abstinence, often undertaken in an isolated place), in a hut he had built himself on this spur of the mountain. His little shelter has been rebuilt at least twice. Once after an earthquake in 1853 and once in the 1990s having lain in ruins for forty years after being blown up in a Soviet anti-religious strike. Nowadays, there is a wooden viewing platform by the house where tourists gather to have their photograph taken looking out over Osh to the Pamirs, which are just visible glinting above a distant haze.

In Babur's house an old Uzbek man prayed while people left charitable offerings of bread and fruit on his windowsill. The old man did not turn or look at us as we crept in and his whispers continued to echo round the whitewashed room. The floor of the room was the bare rock of the mountain polished by centuries of unshod feet, dark grey and reflective like black ice.

Beyond Babur's house, was a shallow scoop in the hillside, which was said to cure backache. It was polished by the constant rubbing of aching backs, and now children whooped as they slid the length of it, and tumbled on top of one another in piles at the bottom. When they saw us they followed us, showing off by swinging from the railings and shouting for our attention. They theatrically demonstrated the curative powers of a hole in the rock for injured hands, while Anna translated, "your hand is broken - your hand is well." Further along, another polished ledge of rock led into a cave supposed to cure headaches. I crawled in with my torch and found it stretched several metres into the mountain.

Mount Sulemein, lying in a line of limestone lumps is said to have the appearance of a reclining pregnant woman and many pilgrims come in the hope of being cured of infertility. Beside the cave, a young mullah read passages from the Koran to an anxious woman. She asked to borrow a sheet of paper from my notebook to write down a particularly important passage and was shown by the mullah how she should hold the paper charm against her stomach. Once we walked on, Anna told me that she had overheard the woman tell the mullah that she had been childless for seven years now, and had come to Sulemein as a last resort. "It has worked for many women. The mountain is very powerful for having children and very famous. It is known that even Benazir Bhutto from Pakistan came here many years ago to pray for a good pregnancy."

Ribbons and strips of cloth were tied to the branches of the trees closest to the path where they bleached in the sun and rain and began to look like blossom. "It is for a wish," Anna told us. "Each ribbon is a wish or for good luck. Many people do this when they visit the mountain." Even Anna had done it although she blushed and refused to tell me when I asked her what she had wished for.

The healing capabilities of the old worn rocks, the ribbons, and the charms were well known to the faithful visitors. These are traditions that survived the secularity of communism. But they are also traditions that have their foundation before Islam when Bronze Age communities nestled in the lee of Sulemein. These villages left evidence of their existence in shamanistic burials and petroglyphs etched onto slabs across the mountain. Sulemein was first of all an animist holy mountain that was subsequently overlaid with a Muslim tradition. This absorption of traditional holy sites (or festivals) by new religions (syncretism) is well documented in other periods of religious transition. Familiar examples are Christmas, the Christian festival which replaced a pagan midwinter feast, and the Kaaba at Mecca, now the centre of Islamic veneration but prior to the sixth century the centre of pagan polytheism. The same thing had happened at both the holy mountains we had already visited. Emei Shan had been a Taoist religious centre before the Buddhists moved in and Kailash had been a Bonnist mountain before the Buddhists took it over by power of numbers (or the talents of a flying monk if the legends are to be believed.)

On Sulemein the impermanence of this holy mountain as a purely Islamic site is stressed in a museum on the south side of the mountain. It is called the "Historical Cultural Museum," a vast cavern, blasted into the rock that curls inwards and upwards to emerge in a triumphant fifty foot high aluminium-flanged portico half way up the mountain. It is a

Soviet-era display and the unsubtle agenda is to put Islam in its place as merely another superstition like the animist beliefs of the Bronze Age. And with Soviet rule, the display suggests, Islam will be consigned to the museum as well. But that was not what happened. Islam survived through communism just as animism survived (in little pieces) through Islam. Like the few Bonnists who still trundle round Kailash noticeable by their anti-clockwise circumambulation, some of the old religious beliefs are still alive on Sulemein. The rocks still cure ailments and provide good luck, the mountain can help you get pregnant, visiting it is a fertility rite. A photograph in the museum shows a female Shaman, who specialised in the treatment of children. She is dressed in ritualistic garments and her tools and talismans lie in front of her: feathers, coins, bones but also a copy of the Koran. Just like the pregnancy mullah we had seen, she was complicit in this collage of old and new, handing out fertility charms from the Koran.

Outside the museum was a wedding party accompanied by a deafening reed pipe and drum combo. It was an Uzbek (and therefore Muslim wedding) but it was also a white wedding (Anna told me this was customary in the urban areas of Kyrgyzstan), with the bride in a puffy meringue dress and the groom in tails. They were at Sulemein for good luck and fertility. Another wedding party arrived half an hour later, it seemed to be a standard part of the ceremony in Osh; not only good luck and fertility but also a spectacular back drop for the wedding photographs.

Anna indicated a point further round the mountain where she told us there was a hole in the rock. Here a husband could insert his wife's head if he suspected her of infidelity – it would stick fast if he was right. There was a high cliff on the top of the mountain from where the guilty wife was thrown if his suspicions were proved correct. It seemed to sum up Sulemein as a mountain of supreme urban convenience. To a shamanistic community it was a shamanistic mountain but when the population became Muslim, the mountain did too, painted anew as the religion washed across the continent. As an Islamic holy mountain it had received the very best of visitors (both Sulemein and Mohammed) – endorsements of the very highest order. It also provided for the everyday needs of the people: cures for illness, treatments for fertility, judgements on a wife's fidelity and the means of execution if she were found guilty.

Further up the mountain Anna showed us the "golden cave," where it was said the bourgeoisie hid their gold during the October revolution. Many were killed before retrieving it and this treasure is said to be still hidden somewhere in the crevices of the rock. Young children clamber about the walls hoping to catch sight of the sparkling rocks, while older ones come to smoke and loiter in the entrance. "Another story," Anna continued, "the mountain covers a great lake. During the Soviet era plans to blow up the entire mountain, and expand Osh into an industrial centre were shelved because of the lake. If the mountain was removed then the lake would be opened and would flood the whole of the fertile Ferghana valley."

We walked down from the cave through the graveyard on its flanks. "There is a story that Sulemein himself is buried on this mountain, although no one knows where." When I looked this up later I could only find that Sulemein was rumoured to be buried in Jerusalem, near the sea of Tiberias, in the Andaman Islands or at the bottom of the ocean in a palace excavated from rock. No mention was made of Mount Sulemein at all, but then no mention had been made of his visit in the first place. Towards the back of the mountain is the footprint of his horse, Abul Ali, now a ghostly horse that clatters around the mountain at night. Perhaps this ghostly horse remains as a symbol for the faithful; Sulemein loved horses and in the Koran, when some particularly beautiful horses were brought before him, he said, "I love good things because they are reminders of my Lord." Several of Anna's friends had seen the ghost rider on the mountain at night, though she agreed with a giggle that the "hangover-free" vodka might well have fuelled these apparitions.

The evening call to prayer floated over as we walked towards the mosque. A small collection of men were washing in a stream (the city water supply was still not working) and the muezzin, his fingers in his ears, his head tilted towards the top of the mountain was calling the faithful to prayer through an intercom microphone attached to the loud-speakers.

"Allahu Akbar, Allahu Akbar…."

*

Rain was tipping down outside. It came in waves, concentrated rain followed by a lull, followed by another hysterical battering. The gutter above our window was blocked and trickles of water wove their way down the window marking clear paths in the dirt, like slug trails. The taps were still dry. We had an early start because our hotel receptionist had told us we needed to register with OVIR, the security police, within three days of our arrival. We were already a day late. We tramped down the soaking street, shoulders hunched against the drips that ran down our necks. In the bank we had three different desks to visit, at the first our requirement was written out onto a chit in triplicate, at the second we paid out money for registration and had the chit stamped, and at the third we got the stamps that would be affixed to our passport. Our clothes quietly dripped on the linoleum floor as they filled out the receipts (a service which cost us a further $0.15 and required a further stamp from a further large frowning woman.) The OVIR office was hidden behind an adult education building, staffed by a doorman who had never heard of OVIR. Having at last found the correct OVIR office, we were sent back to the adult education building to have our passports copied and the doorman told us there was no photocopier in the building. We returned to the OVIR office and they told us it was on the second floor. The doorman shrugged when we told him this. Finally, our visas were stamped with a green stamp. It had taken us four hours and we were completely soaked.

There was still no water in the taps of Osh. I wondered if there ever would be. We left the Allay hotel that afternoon slightly embarrassed by the smell of our unflushed toilet that now seemed to extend along most of the corridor. At midday we picked up a taxi, it was a Lada with a windscreen damaged so long ago that elongated communities of algae were forming in the cracks. The smell of rotten eggs got stronger and stronger as we drove. This was to become familiar as all the private cars produced the same odour, I think due to the impurities in the petrol, which is sold in plastic bottles at roadside stalls. As we skirted the Uzbek border on the road north to Jalal Abad the rain stopped and shafts of light shone through the cloud lighting up the fields of the Ferghana valley.

*

The Jalal Abad Sanatorium nestles in almond groves overlooking the town and is famous for its mineral baths. We could not have been more in need of mineral baths than after waterless Osh, and the first thing we did was to catch a taxi to the hilltop sanatorium. The road wound up in hairpin bends through a forest of low, gnarled almond trees. Wrought iron gates led into a circle of buildings, which might once have been grand. The staff were sitting around the buildings, bottles in hands and greeted us with the words, "Closed for three days. You want vodka?"

It was the 125th anniversary of the town and the staff had been given a holiday to allow them to join the festivities. We had gone for six days unwashed. Now, in this spa town, which exported water across the country, the baths were closed. However, we knew better than to get involved in a mid-afternoon vodka session and walked back to our hotel where we took brief and unsatisfying cold showers (the electricity was not on during daylight hours).

We ate dinner next to the table where the winner of the 125th anniversary wrestling match was celebrating his victory. Returning from the toilet he seemed to lose the way to his own table and slumped down at ours, ordering vodka, despite our protests and excuses. Of course, no excuse was good enough and we were taken upstairs to join the dance. The wrestler's unfortunate wife held him up while he stumbled around the dance floor in a lolling waltz and when the tempo quickened he skipped in front of the mirror, as if he were warming up for yet another bout, fixing himself with an admiring stare. Toast followed toast – to us, to Scotland – from us, to Kyrgyz hospitality – from everyone to international friendship. The wrestler slumped in his chair, his conversation for the next hour was to point to each of us and repeat our name and then to repeat his own name to himself. "Sie-mon, Eee-on… Mohammed." It was strange that he seemed to have most trouble remembering his own, but reminded us each time that Mohammed was like Mohammed Ali who was a great sportsman and a good Muslim just like him.

CHAPTER 10

North

The town of Arslanbob is spread out over two small river valleys that meet just below the main square. Each house is surrounded by a few acres of smallholding - a field, a vegetable garden and a few fruit trees. Like many towns in the Ferghana valley, it is populated almost entirely by ethnic Uzbeks caught in the wrong country by border decisions made in Moscow. We made our way up to the house of Ibrahim, the village German teacher, who, we were told, had a room to rent. The path to his house ran parallel with the river and directly in front of us was the misted foothills of Babash Ata, tongues of snow advancing down the scree. Tiny mill-houses clung to the banks or squatted over man-made channels that cut away from the river, where water foamed round wooden sluices and water wheels. A sturdy concrete bridge took us over the river to the rows of empty pens where the Thursday animal market was held. Ibrahim's house lay in the shelter of fruit trees on the gentle slopes of the valley. The garden was irrigated by a tiny stream, which could be diverted to whichever vegetable patch or tree needed water. Hens scratched around the porch and a cow dumbly pondered our arrival.

Afternoon tea - almond cake, jam sponge and delicious home made bread covered with honey, jam, fresh butter and bowls of raisins and walnuts - came laid out on a cloth on the outdoor bed which looked over the double valleys of Arslanbob. We sat there all afternoon until the lights came on across the valley, illuminating the windows of irregularly spaced houses lying at the centre of their own simple patchworks of fields and trees.

The room Ibrahim rented to visitors was separate from the house, in its own little block across the garden. Next to it was the visitors' dining room with a low table and long cylindrical cushions lying against the wall, and in a corrugated plastic cubicle behind the block was a warm shower. In the evenings Ibrahim filled up the roof tank (already warmed by the day's sun) with hot water from the stove - the first warm shower we had had in Kyrgyzstan.

The next day Ibrahim took us up towards the base of Babash Ata. Above the river valley of Arslanbob the ground flattened, giving way to fields and trees and we waited while Ibrahim visited the "high garden." He came back with his bag full of apples, which we peeled and ate in the morning sun. A few were large and sweet cultivated apples but most were wild and bitter like quinces. A man passed us on horseback and told Ibrahim there was horse training going on in the higher fields, which we might like to watch. A goat had been killed especially. I wondered why a goat needed to be killed for horse training, but as we climbed to the higher fields it became clear they were training the horses by playing a variant of the game of buzkashi. This is a traditionally Afghan game involving two mounted teams who fight over a calf or goat carcass and try to carry it over the line at the opposite end of the pitch. This was an informal version; there were no teams and the only purpose was to put the horses through their paces with the added interest of throwing a dead goat around. The goat was decapitated and placed in the centre of the field. The horsemen leaned off their saddles to pick up the carcass and raced around the field, pursued by a dozen other riders. They galloped alongside the goat carrier and attempted to wrest it from where it lay on his saddle, while their horses continued at full speed. If the rider kept a hold of the goat he galloped on, whooping, a full circuit of the field, his whip between his teeth, the white headless body flapping on the pommel of his saddle.

We stood with the resting riders and took photographs of the charging horses in that amphitheatre of mountains. We were encouraged to join in but it would have been a lethal undertaking for an inexperienced rider. If we were not thrown from the saddle by these hyperactive animals we would probably have been knocked out by the flying goat.

The horses' sweat rose in foam from where the bridle rubbed against their hide and their eyes rolled as they tongued the bit. The riders were white knuckled and panting, their faces powdered with dust that stuck to their sweat. "Afterwards they will eat the goat," Ibrahim told us, "the meat will be... beautiful."

As we climbed, Ibrahim told us the legend of the village.

There was an extremely hardworking man called Arslanbob who served the prophet Mohammed. The prophet appreciated his modesty and earnestness so as a reward he sent Arslanbob away to find a beautiful and comfortable place, a paradise on the earth, where he might settle. Arslanbob passed through many countries searching for such a place until he came across this idyllic valley in what is now Kyrgyzstan. It was a picturesque place with a foaming mountain river, good soil, and climate, but it lacked trees. Hearing of it, the Prophet sent Arslanbob a big sack of seeds. Arslanbob took this bag and climbed to the top of the highest mountain and scattered its contents over the whole valley. Trees sprang up and transformed the valley into a huge garden, and ever since the mountain has been called Babash Ata, which means the beginning of the garden.

Ibrahim moved his arm round in an arc with the mountain at his back as if he were scattering the seeds, pointing out the individual fields where his seeds had landed: "apple, plum, apricot, pistachio, almond, walnut, potatoes, corn, apples, pears, cabbages, sunflowers. You need never go hungry in Arslanbob." But it was not just the seeds that the prophet sent; it was the land that Arslanbob had chosen. It was an incredibly rich soil and Ibrahim held up his fingers to demonstrate, they were stained a purple black. "It is from the iodine. When we take off the walnut casings we get the iodine on our fingers." On the other side of the mountain by Toktogul Reservoir they cannot grow walnuts; the soil is lacking in the vital nutrients, and the people have historically suffered from goitre, a condition caused by lack of iodine in the diet. They had not been blessed with the foresight of the Prophet's tireless helper, Arslanbob.

Higher up we could see the acres of walnut groves, which are the provider of Arslanbob's chief export. Each family is given a plot of walnut trees and must deliver 60% of the crop to the government every harvest. The reason that Ibrahim (the German teacher) was able to accompany us today was because Arslanbob's school has an unofficial two week holiday in the autumn to allow the children to gather the walnuts. That evening Ibrahim's son returned from the family groves with seventy kilograms of walnuts in his saddle bags, and the family sat in the garden well past dusk rustling the papery casings from the shells and talking to one another in soft strains of Uzbeki.

We carried on climbing the flanks of Babash Ata until we could go no further; a high cliff blocked our way. Down the centre streamed a waterfall, falling from a crack for eighty metres and battering against a gravel-filled pool. Above us, Ibrahim pointed out two eagles, soaring gracefully through a mist of spray with upturned wing tips. A wire fence ran along the top of the ravine, covered in ribbons of fabric tied in little knots, just as we had seen on Mount Sulemein.

"Newly married people come here. They tie a knot - it is good for children," Ibrahim told us. When I pressed him about the origins of this belief he answered, "It is for good luck. It is a custom, a tradition." Arslanbob is a relatively strict Muslim community; the women dress particularly modestly wearing loose trousers under their skirts rather than the thick tights considered enough in most of the country. And yet despite this Islamic orthodoxy, the animist traditions that I had seen practised on Mount Sulemein survive here too and were extremely popular judging from the sheer number of ribbons tied to the fence. I asked if Ibrahim had tied a knot here. "Of course," he replied. He did, after all, have five healthy children.

*

On our third day in Arslanbob we were invited to Ibrahim's nephew's wedding. "When I was young, the whole village would come to weddings, but now it is too big, so only relations come." This did not limit numbers too much as Ibrahim was related to about half of the village.

Ibrahim's cousin's smallholding lay a few fields away. Ibrahim had changed out of the long leather boots and rubber galoshes that he wore for walking and now wore polished leather shoes and his best suit. His felt homberg was replaced with a white straw hat with a black band. It was late afternoon and the air in the garden was warm and smelled of fruit. Groups milled around the apple trees or sat cross-legged on the grass. On a paved area, two pots of plauv bubbled - supported over fires on a triangle of concrete blocks. A singer with taped backing music had set up his amplifier on an outdoor bed and was hollering old favourites over two speakers one of which was suspended from the branches of a tree. Three kids sat next to the speaker wide-eyed and swaying, but otherwise he was being ignored.

We were shown to an outdoor seating platform, canopied and spread with a table cloth, while steaming plates of plauv and laghman (meat stew and noodles), and bowls of walnuts were set before us. There was an old man already sitting there whom Ibrahim introduced as his father. He was eighty-five years old but there was an animation in his manner, which made him appear far younger. We had seen people who looked older and more wizened than him in villages across Asia and they often turned out to be only in their sixties but prematurely aged by the sun and hard work. Here was a man who was old by any standards but in remarkably good shape. He told us his father (Ibrahim's grandfather) had lived to one hundred and two and put this health and longevity down to Arslanbob's walnuts. "When you squeeze a walnut you can see the oil come out. Our body needs this oil like a machine needs oil to run smoothly. Without it we grow rusty and we cannot move. The walnut is also good for our brain too, it keeps the brain alive."

Ibrahim leaned towards us, "It is a very religious wedding. I do not find it very interesting. Very, very traditional." He shook his head sadly. There was an abrupt separation of the sexes: the woman all sat around the house, a blaze of brightly coloured Uzbek headscarves, while the men milled around the garden, or sat cross legged beneath the apple trees.

As soon as the food arrived, the vodka toasts began. The vodka was swiftly decanted from bottle to teapot and the bottle was hidden under the tablecloth. Large measures were poured from the teapot into tea bowls. I presumed this surreptitious disguise of the vodka was because it was "a very religious wedding." After two bowls, Ibrahim began to confide in us.

"That is his father, my cousin," he nodded towards a round-bellied drunk-looking man. "The father is not happy. His other three sons had normal weddings, like my son had, where everyone is sitting together around a table and then everyone is dancing together. But this is his fourth son and he and his friends are very religious." He motioned again to the father of the groom who had also been drinking from the teapot and was now swaying slightly to the professional karaoke singer. He beamed at us when he saw us looking towards him. He didn't look obviously unhappy; he looked dangerously close to falling into the pot of plauv.

"But he is my nephew so we toast him with vodka for his happiness." The tea-bowls were refilled to the brim all round. We drank and bit into slices of sweet melon to take away the taste.

Several toasts later the bride arrived, in the ubiquitous Lada. Groups of women crowded round the car doors and passed piles of flat bread wrapped in coloured scarves, bowls of yoghurt and packets of salt through the window. "These are the basic foods that we must have to survive, they will bring the family prosperity and mean that they will never go hungry."

There was a delay as the bride's family bus had broken down at the bottom of the hill, and they arrived on foot over the next ten minutes smiling and out of breath. We had reached the climax of the party. The karaoke machine was turned off and a long brass horn, which stretched at least two metres, gave off a deep percussive blast, accompanied by a drum. The groom, in a long black velvet coat and black and white skullcap opened the door of the Lada and put a brown blanket over the bride's head. The horn had only one note, but with the mounting excitement, the blasts came louder and faster. The drum rattled. The covered bride was lifted onto the groom's shoulder and carried into the house where she was set down among the other women. The groom ran straight back outside to his group of friends, and smoked a little and drank tea (and for him it was tea.) That was the only contact the bride and groom would have that day. She was now in the company of the other women indoors and the groom carried on chatting to his friends.

As it got dark, the men began to dance in the courtyard, twirling round, arms outstretched, red-faced and sweating in the muggy evening. Those watching tucked small Som notes under their caps and clapped in time to the music, urging the dancers to ever more daring skips and turns. The horn had been replaced by the singer and every song speeded up at the end, so that the dancers twirled faster and faster, the white designs on their hats blurring with the speed of their pirouettes. As a close relative, Ibrahim took his turn on the floor early and called his father over, who danced less flamboyantly than the younger men, but with a stately precision, that suggested these were the *correct* steps - dancing on walnut-oiled joints...

The women watched amusedly from the safety of the terrace.

*

We stayed longer than we had planned at Arslanbob. On the outdoor bed, propped up with cushions, looking over the rolling patchwork of hills we cracked walnuts and didn't talk about leaving. The water ran one way or the other, into the vegetable patch or to the plum tree and everything grew effortlessly in the russet-green warmth of this idyllic valley. Of course I knew the reality; Ibrahim told me about the winter when the snow fell so deep he had to dig out his horse, he told me his wage which wasn't enough to feed a family, and of the helplessness the previous year when his wife had fallen ill so far away from a hospital. But even with these troubles he loved this land and his village with a parental pride and it was easy to see why.

It wasn't just the perfection of Arslanbob that delayed us. We just felt like lingering more. At the outset we had moved frantically; twenty-four hour train journeys, mad rushes from mountain to airport - and how I had seethed at the delay in going west from Lhasa! Partly it was a hangover from living in London where everything had to be done with the greatest possible urgency. Initially I couldn't quite believe that this new existence was possible.

Now the anxiety that made me cover too many miles in one day suddenly lifted and sitting on the outdoor bed in Arslanbob I felt something I had not felt for a very long time –

that this time was mine, and there was plenty more where it came from.

Looking back on it, I see that the change in the rhythm of our journey had come gradually, but it was in Arslanbob that I first noticed it. Simon noticed it too and when I suggested we stay a couple more days he smiled with his wide grin and closed his eyes. "Good idea." Then we smoked the cigarettes that we had been given as presents at the wedding and lay on the cushions until the sun left to light up another valley and the air turned cold. Inside, dinner had been laid out on the low table lit by a gas lantern – meat, rice and walnuts. Ibrahim, having already eaten in the kitchen was lying against the cushions ready to tell us another story.

*

We set off in darkness in a remarkably new Lada for the two-day journey to Karakol in North Eastern Kyrgyzstan. Although we were on the main road from Osh to the capital Bishkek, long piles of hay took up one and sometimes both lanes, the farmers taking precedence over the drivers in the rush to dry the harvest before winter. Normally we drove round the hay but if another car was on the road we drove straight through it. Sometimes there would be patches of grain spread on the tarmac too, guarded from prowling hens by children with sticks. The road here did not see much traffic and was treated as an extension of the farmyard.

For a while we followed the Naryn River, a green stretch of water set against banks, which were powdery red like a Martian canal. It was a striking combination, like colours on a flag, and it seemed uncanny that such bright contrasting colours should lie together and not dissolve into a muddy brown. The Naryn swelled to a thin cobalt lake before tightening again in the mountains, where the road carved into the cliff.

Back on the plains we passed an animal market; a field of bobbing black and white hats in a haze of dust kicked up by the livestock. Goats were being dragged along the road by their new owners and stored in the boots of Ladas where they stared at us through the horizontal slits of their pupils.

The Lada struggled up the bends to the Al Abel pass where we crossed the snow line. A little later, we passed a village entirely made of old railway carriages raised on stones. There had never been a railway track across this pass; these carriages were brought by road to this high place to create a pre-fabricated village. They looked incongruous with their once bright paintwork now peeling and their rusted axles propped up, as if awaiting repairs. In some places the slats had rotted away exposing plastic patching like the soft skin under a turtle's shell. With roaming bands of dogs and children playing around them, these carriages might have been the vehicles of travelling people, although, wheelless and rotting, these would never move again. The children stopped to watch us pass then resumed their game of teasing the dogs. I asked the driver what the isolated village was called.

"No name," he replied.

"Why do the people live there?"

He shrugged.

I wondered what had brought them to their snowbound, peeling village. There was no work here, no industry. Cars passed through but did not stop. It did not even have a name.

There was another pass and a long tunnel, then we were freewheeling down the mountains again in neutral. The sky darkened and we slowed down so as to not come to grief on the now invisible potholes.

*

We waited two hours for the private bus from Bishkek to Karakol to fill up completely before it left. We were wedged in with the multiple bags of our fellow passengers that we had become used to on our Asian bus journeys. Hessian sacks of potatoes clogged the leg space between the seats and the central aisle was knee deep in rolls of roofing felt. Other packages were bulkily wrapped in padded plastic, their contents a mystery. It was hot inside the bus and I slept fitfully, head lolling on the vibrating glass. We stopped for lunch in Toru Aigyr, where we could see the blue Issyk Kul Lake through the lines of poplars, and above the shore, the large decrepit buildings of a Soviet-era sanatorium. We ate manti, doughy parcels of pastry wrapped around fatty mutton and drank koumys, a drink made from fermented mare's milk. It tasted like a runny yoghurt with a hint of yeast and the old woman selling it told us it was a cure for terrible diseases that I could not even find in my Russian dictionary.

Our journey ended in twilight for the second day running. Lights were going on in the windows of the columns of flats which surrounded Karakol bus stop. They were dreary buildings, all six of them the same height, facing the same direction, the same shade of institutional concrete grey. Beyond them the other blocks were low rise but similarly anonymous and decrepit - the dreary results of expansion during Soviet times. They looked lost in this sombre wilderness. To the West lay Lake Issyk Kul under an almost full moon. When the wind blew, the reflections clouded and the water darkened to an inky blue, but when it was still, the whole surface glowed. On the other side, Karakol was hemmed in by the mountains of the Tian Shan, with dead shadows of forests in the lower reaches and a luminescence of gleaming snow-covered tops. "The snow that has accumulated here since the creation of the world has changed into ice rocks, that do not melt in either spring or summer," wrote one early traveller[14] to these mountains, "there is a strong cold wind and travellers are molested by dragons."

The bus terminal emptied quickly, the passengers hurrying off under their sacks and rolls of luggage. After the mugginess of the bus I shivered in the cold air. The streets were silent.

*

The gate man at the Karakol animal market was doing good business. He held up a wedge of notes to show me, ten Som per animal, and they had been arriving since two in the morning. Men and livestock make the overnight trek in time for trading to start at 4 am. The previous night the clocks had gone back and I imagined them in that extra hour of waiting, stamping their feet in the cold of a cloudless night.

Rain had been spitting all morning and the sky was overcast. This market was unpleasantly cold, unlike the dust and sweat of the Uighur markets. Thin curtains of light material with incongruous nursery patterns had been put around the food stalls to cut out some of the wind. But still, smoke from the oil-can stoves blew in every direction and the

---

[14] Xuan Zang, the seventh century Chinese traveller.

cooks closed their eyes against it, stirring their pots at arm's length as their customers crouched on their haunches.

The animals stood, expressionless and motionless while streams of men wove through them, their black and white hats bobbing like bouys in the sea. Some hats were tall and peaked like cones, some rounder like scull caps, some had the curling embroidery designs picked out in white on white felt, elegant albino versions of the original hat. The mood of the market seemed to be reflected in the weather, subdued and miserable, with few deals going on. It was already mid-morning; maybe it was too late.

On the fringes of the market, past the lines of fat-tailed sheep, and the cows standing hoof-deep in the mud bath of the centre, two men hammered shoes onto a horse held steady in a cradle of wood and rope. They took opposite hooves and secured them before racing each other to finish, tapping nails around the shoe and nipping the ends off with pliers. Further along was the piglet market. They slept in the boots of Ladas, presented on a bed of straw, or peeked out of wooden boxes which sat on trolleys. When bought, the squealing animals were wrestled into sacks and slung, wriggling and squeaking over their new owner's shoulder.

I had not seen pigs in the animal markets of the south, which was probably because of the high numbers of ethnic Uzbeks, who take a stricter line on Islam. As a growing town in the North East of the country, the ethnic traditions of Karakol are more diluted. Soviet industrial programmes brought Christian immigrants from Russia and the Ukraine to work in Karakol's industry and in the mines of the Tian Shan Mountains and they brought with them their own eating habits and culture.

We stayed in a guest house, run by the self-appointed Ukrainian community leader, Valentin, who had the responsibility of running the small library of Ukrainian language books and newspapers donated by the Ukrainian ambassador in Bishkek. He was different in accent and appearance from his Kyrgyz neighbours, with light, sandy hair, slate blue eyes, and a bulbous nose. "When the ambassador comes from Bishkek, he tells me that when they build industry here, they bring in Ukrainians because everyone knows they are good at work. So we are proud to be here. This place is, you know, a little bit of Ukraine and it is our happy home."

When we went climbing in the Tian Shan mountains, it was Valentin's Ukrainian apprentice guide who took us. Valentin judged the local yurts to be unsatisfactory and had built his own hut in the mountains with the flue of the stove diverted under the sleeping platform, similar to the incorporation of the stove in the sleeping area of Siberian peasant houses. Nearby were the scorching hot sulphurous pools of Altyn Rashan. On Slavic's instruction we jumped into the river that ran through snow covered banks, then limped, swearing, back across the gravel and ice and plunged into the hot pools, our legs pricked by hundred of pins.

"He is a good man to work for," Slavic told me as we trudged back to the hut, exhausted by the extremes of temperature. "I came here three years ago, when I was fourteen. My mother sent me here, because this is where my grandmother lives. There is nothing for me now in the Ukraine. Here there will be work for the tourists and that is good money. Stok Kangri, Pik Pebonka, Pik Lenin," he listed the famous high mountains of Kyrgyzstan. More and more western climbers were coming every year, to the great ranges of the country that had been inaccessible to Westerners until the break-up of the Soviet Union and Kyrgyz independence in 1990. "I work for Valentin for five years maybe and he will teach me how to be a guide. Then I can work for climbers and tourists. I have already climbed Pik Pabonka. It was in the summer. We had no ropes, no helmets, no ice axes. Two or three times I was close to death. I fell up to here," he motioned to his armpits, "in a crevasse. But we were dreaming about climbing it all the winter."

Kyrgyzstan is not rich in oil like its neighbours Uzbekistan, and Kazakhstan. It has some mining but its only significant natural resource is water, which is unlikely to drive major growth. The economic future of the country will rest on tourism. The flow of immigrants to Karakol that began with Soviet work-force requirements has continued with the promising pull of tourist jobs, which is a good sign for Kyrgyzstan's future.

Near Valentin's guesthouse was the entirely wooden Russian Orthodox cathedral built in 1895 to replace the stone cathedral, destroyed in an earthquake. The structure was complete with new tin domes replaced in the 1990s when the building became a cathedral again, after decades of use as a gentleman's club for Soviet officials and the military. Inside, the air smelt of varnish, and the boards creaked in dull protest as I walked up the nave. At the end of the chancel hung the icon of the Gentle Virgin Mary, illuminated by the light from a long uncleaned window. The rectangular icon stood about one and a half metres high with a cerulean blue background and showed the Gentle Virgin in a gold dress holding the Christ Child in a matching outfit. Both of them were crowned with rays of light and the Virgin had an additional white jewelled crown on her head. The Virgin observed me with a contemplative and sympathetic gaze but with her face turned slightly to one side as if in submission. The Christ Child looked more aloof and his gaze did not connect but looked somewhere over the top of the empty pews as if he were concerned with more important things.

I could see a few pockmarks around the chest and shoulder of the virgin, but the faces of both figures were in excellent condition. During the anti-Russian uprising of 1916, the icon hung nearby in the Svelty Mys monastery and, it is said, repelled the bullets of rebel soldiers while shining with an ethereal light. When the soldiers left the monastery, the Gentle Virgin shed tears of blood for the monks murdered in the attack. Even today the icon is revered among the Christian Russian and Ukrainian population as having supernatural qualities, and copies of it are said to have healing powers.

On Sunday morning I looked back into the cathedral. It was illuminated with candles that ran along the sides of the pews like landing lights and the sweet smoke of incense hung in the air. At the transept stood two family groups huddled round two babies clad in long, white baptismal gowns – a new generation of the Russo-Ukrainian population. I closed the door quietly not wanting to disturb them.

*

We sped down the south coast of Issyk Kul in our Lada taxi, Bon Jovi in the car stereo and all the windows open to the fresh wind that streamed off the lake. Here Issyk Kul was the light blue of washed-out denim fading into a white mist that obscured the far shore and made the toothy ridges of the Tian Shan float disembodied above the horizon. The road was fringed with autumn trees: avenues of poplars, yellow and lit-up above dark trunks like rows of giant roman candles; stumpy pollarded trees, coming alive in the wind like disco balls and sending showers of golden leaves into the air. There was an excitement and optimism in this riot of tumbling colours and reflected light; everything was vibrant that morning as though the very leaves were defying the prospect of winter with a final burst of colour as they blew away to die. Bon Jovi belted out songs from other decades, *"gonna live while I'm alive, sleep when I'm dead..."* I sat with an elbow on the window and grinned into the wind.

At Barskoon a broad dusty track led up into the mountains to gold mines run by Kumtor, a Kyrgyz-Canadian joint venture. We followed a lorry which wheezed up the gradual incline, spraying water from a hose at its rear to keep down the dust on the access road. A few kilometres up, we left the taxi and climbed through steep forest to the waterfall, tumbling down from a west-facing cliff. In the shadow of the surrounding hills the waterfall was beginning to freeze into a rounded bole at the base and would be completely solid by winter. Huge firs surrounded the waterfall, and as I got closer I could see the lower branches were covered with tiny fabric knots; here was another impressive natural phenomenon with the power to make wishes come true.

Further along the south shore of Issyk Kul is the river gorge of Tamga, which cuts at right angles away from the shore and is the site of the Tamga Tash (Letter Stone). On a grassy bank, with the river tumbling far below, lies a large boulder, like an open egg split length-wise almost exactly in half, revealing its smooth inner surfaces. On the outer surface of both halves of the rock are Tibetan Sanskrit inscriptions carved in heavy relief, yet rounded by centuries of weathering and blurred by lichen. "Om me padme Om," reads the 1,500 year old Buddhist mantra, together with a carved image of the lotus flower.

Sitting on a promontory above the lake, the letter stone has an impressive perspective. Buddhists chose situations like this as sacred places deriving power from the abstract beauty of symmetrical rocks and cliffs and the impact of huge vistas.

Before the arrival of Islam there is evidence that a number of different religions, Zoroastrian, Nestorian Christian, Manichean and Buddhist, co-existed in this area lying as it does in the heart of Asia, criss-crossed by the ebb and flow of religious influences along the Silk Road. Early maps located a thirteenth century Nestorian monastery enshrining the corpse of St Matthew at the eastern end of Issyk Kul, and Zoroastrian tombs and evidence of Manichean communities have been discovered in several places close to the lake. North west of the lake at Krasnaya Rechka lie the remains of a Buddhist temple and Buddhist cemetery; an indication of how established this religion from the East used to be in Kyrgyzstan.

Two bushy hawthorn saplings grew right beside the cleft rock. Intertwined among their russet leaves was a secondary plumage of knotted material tied the length of the branches. It was the same as we had seen on Sulemein, by the waterfalls on Babash Ata and an hour before at the Barskoon waterfall, each fabric knot sealing a wish. However, this site was explicitly Buddhist; it had not been converted to the Islamic tradition, like Sulemein, and it was not a harmless natural phenomenon like a waterfall. It was a man-made, Buddhist holy place, and yet it still attracted devotion from the Muslim population who made mini-pilgrimages to the Sanskrit-covered rock to make their wishes with material knots. The survival of old beliefs in new religions is far from being peculiar to Kyrgyzstan and yet one cannot help feeling that these proud, independently-minded communities with their nomadic background in mountain and steppe were particularly determined to adapt Islam to their terms. It seemed to me that Kyrgyz Islam had remained unconventional, integrating an older non-Quoranic set of beliefs.

In politics as well as religion a cultural tenacity informed the Kyrgyz adoption of new ideas. The collectivisation programme of the 1920s and 30s was completely incompatible with the traditional nomadic lifestyle of large portions of the population. Collectivisation required one unit of workers to manage an area of land all year round. It could not accommodate the process of migration and the concept of common grazing on the jailoo. The herders accepted other Soviet-imposed policies but they would not accept collectivisation and many slaughtered their flocks and fled to China in reaction against it. I had met descendants of these emigrants in the Karakorums a month earlier. Their reaction seemed to be part of a characteristic conservatism common to mountain dwellers all over the world. In high places wariness towards new ideas is, I suppose, necessary when the margins of survival are tight and the impact of making even moderate changes in lifestyle could be fatal.

We stood on the lakeside waiting for the bus to Bishkek, and in the clear water we could see the rocks several feet below. Specks of white far from the shore were the Issyk Kul swans, which migrate from Siberia to winter on the lake that never freezes. A man brought a group of seven horses down to the shore and they danced along the beach. Bridleless, against the untouched backdrop of the lake, they could have been wild.

Bishkek was a civilised city, with broad tree-lined avenues and parks, now ankle deep in russet leaves. Although the architecture was still in the triumphal Soviet vein, it was stately rather than austere. On one side of the wide central street, Chui Prospekt, ran a line of arched arcades - shops on the street level and government offices in the upper stories. On the other side were the main administrative buildings, the "White House" set behind formal gardens and a huge semi-circle of flags from all over the world. Next to it was the massive façade of the National Historical Museum, overlooking an equally large paved square where the new crimson and gold flag of the country flapped, guarded every hour of the day by two soldiers standing at attention. Beside the flag stood a statue of Lenin, high on a plinth, outstretched hand raised as if preaching to the circle of snowy peaks that overlook the Kyrgyz capital. The statue had not been pulled down at independence and seemed to represent a tolerant acceptance of history (or maybe it was another manifestation of the cautious Kyrgyz attitude to too much change all at once.)

On the top floor of the National Historical Museum the Kyrgyz nomadic tradition was celebrated in a recent display, while on the floor below there remained the Soviet-era display of imitation bronze casts. These lined the whole room in a 360-degree frieze and told the story of the proletarian revolution and its victory over the bourgeoisie. The statues were getting old now and occasionally a hand or a worker's shovel had been damaged revealing white crumbling plaster and a wire skeleton under the bronze coloured paint. No one could be bothered to patch them up anymore.

Bishkek had a cosmopolitan air like nowhere else in the country. We ate 24 hour breakfasts and milkshakes on the outdoor tables of "Fatboys Diner," surprised by the lines of girls on their way to the university in calf length boots and mini skirts. In the evening we retired to "The Pub" where we drank pilsner brewed by an expat German. For dinner, we picked from burger bars, Chinese, Indian, Italian, French and a cosy little Polish place where the waitress changed into a belly dancing outfit after we had finished our main course and gyrated around the tables before changing back into her apron again and serving us coffee. In one of the new clubs which had sprung up along Chui Prospekt there was a live band that sang classics from the eighties, "Summer of 'Sixty-nine" and "Final Countdown." Their lead singer was the only Kyrgyz I have seen with dreadlocks that tumbled from his Rastafarian wool hat.

The week before we reached the city, Kofi Annan, then Secretary General of the UN, had visited and stayed for five days of meetings, and the local English language newspaper, the "Central Asian Times," trumpeted this as a milestone of the country's progress. As a young vulnerable country, Kyrgyzstan has made the decision to tie itself firmly to America and has made land available for a large American air base outside Bishkek's Manas airport to accommodate up to 3,000 soldiers. Unlike the strategic US bases in Uzbekistan and Tajikistan, the US is empowered to use the Kyrgyz base for whatever purpose it chooses, including launching of an attack on a foreign power.

Allied forces involved in the Afghan war used the air base near Bishkek and there seemed to be a continuing presence. On our first night in "The Pub" (or the "American Bar" as the taxi drivers call it) we met one of the allied troops who was involved with air patrols over Afghanistan. He was very tall and fair with an extreme short back and sides that left a toothbrush effect on the top of his head. He was part of the Dutch air force, and his job was to plan the flight routes across Afghanistan, which provide support to the special forces teams on the ground. It was his birthday, and he called to us from across the bar that we must come and celebrate with him. He had come into town with a friend from his unit but the friend had fallen asleep in a toilet cubicle downstairs and now he was all alone.

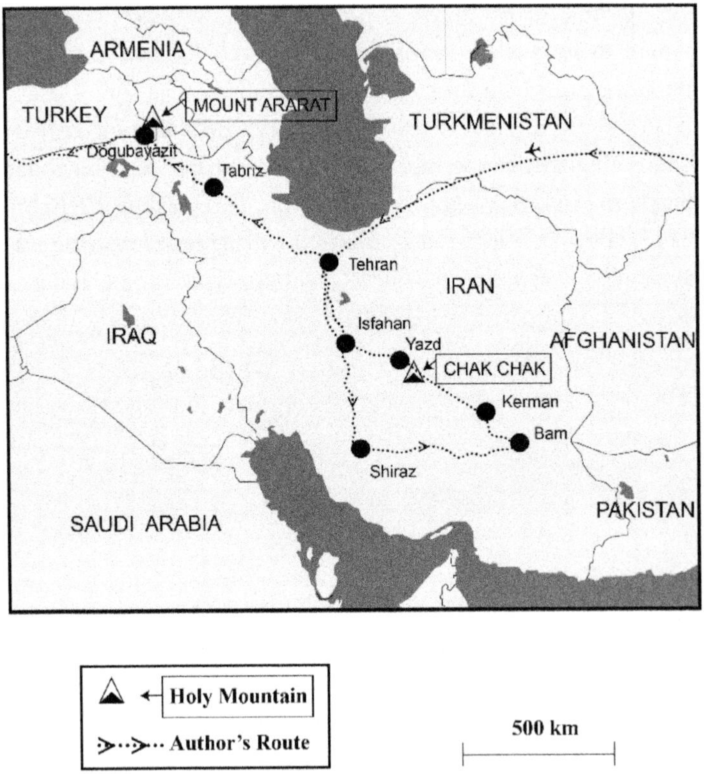
ARMENIA
TURKEY
MOUNT ARARAT
TURKMENISTAN
Dogubayazit
Tabriz
Tehran
IRAN
IRAQ
Isfahan
Yazd
AFGHANISTAN
CHAK CHAK
Kerman
Bam
Shiraz
PAKISTAN
SAUDI ARABIA
Holy Mountain
Author's Route
500 km

CHAPTER 11

Iran

We flew from Kyrgyzstan to Iran. The overland journey would have required at least two further Central Asian visas and coordinating the timing of these was too complex. We arrived late at night in Tehran airport and waited for the early flight South to Shiraz. Slumped in an airport chair reading the newspaper late in the evening I realized there had been a flaw in our planning. We had arrived in Iran, the most strictly observant of all the Muslim countries we would travel to, on the second day of Ramadam. At the airport, the cafes were closing up for dawn, having served Sahur, Ramadan breakfast, at 5 in the morning. However, in the departure lounge tea was still being served in the café, which was concealed from the rest of the departure lounge behind a screen.

"Ramadan…" a suited fellow passenger told us nodding at the screen. Seeing we were still confused he continued, "During Ramadan, people cannot eat in daylight hours. But if you are a traveller then you must eat, this is also an Islamic law. All travellers who leave before the mid-day prayers and travel more than 22.5 kilometres have to break their Ramadan fast. But when they do this, they must not eat or drink or smoke *in front of those* who are fasting. They must do it hidden. That is why the café is hidden." I had not known how detailed the regulations on Ramadan were. The suited gentleman introduced himself. "I am Raza Khan, I am an insurance executive." His English was accented but precise, his suit looked expensive and he wore gold cufflinks on his double cuffed shirt. He opened his briefcase and pulled out the annual report of his company to show us the picture of him and his partners on the inside cover. There were four brothers, grouped around a dark wood desk where a white haired man was sitting, hands clasped, gold spectacles and smiling. "My father." The backdrop was shelves of plain spined books. I noticed the bright cover of the self-help business book, "Harvard Course in Business," amidst his other papers as he replaced the report. He pulled out another book, a Farsi-English dictionary of insurance terms, "I am the author," he announced proudly, "it is the first bilingual dictionary of insurance terminology ever written."

I didn't know how to reply.

"What do you think of our country?" he fixed me with a penetrating stare.

"Lovely… friendly," I offered back.

"No, no, I mean our state, our leaders?" This was even more difficult. We had only just arrived and were understandably nervous about getting into a political discussion. What balanced comments could one make about a religious dictatorship, a parliament which could be over-ruled by the unelected supreme leader, courts dominated by clerics?

"I will tell you, there is *no good* leadership here. A country like this is rich, yes, it has resources, rich, rich resources, we can be rich. We have a great capacity for *wealth creation*. But the management has no credibility. There is no belief in them. They should inspire confidence, but they do not. They should lead us from the front by reflecting our aspirations, but they are apart. It is a defunct leadership. It will soon be quite impotent."

He continued on this vein for twenty minutes peppering his tirade with management jargon straight from the Harvard Business course. "We were a great empire, huge, *fully functioning*. The greatest, most powerful Empire in the world. You can see this in our monuments."

We would see the greatest monument later that day at Persepolis, the old Achaemenid capital, a forest of columns and vast gateways set high on a promontory an hour from Shiraz. The staircases of the palace sloped gently so visiting dignitaries could glide up and down gracefully and the sides were covered with carvings showing just how expansive this empire was. The figures stood in lines that were piled on top of each other and showed all the different subject races of the Achaemenid emperor; Ethiopians, Indians, Arabs, Thracians, Parthians, Cappadocians, Elamites and Medians with spices, gold, donkeys, camels, giraffes all brought as tribute. There was a similar display of continental dominance this time by a later Persian dynasty at the nearby site of Naqsh-e Rostam. A high relief frieze shows the victory of the Sassanian King, Sharpur I, over the Roman invader, the Emperor Valerian, who kneels suppliantly showing his respect with the traditional upraised finger. Raza Khan was quite right: the extent of the Persian Empire had been quite phenomenal.

"But now we are introverted," he continued, "and the people are claustrophobic. Men cannot travel abroad before they have completed their two years military service and even after this they find it difficult to travel to Europe and America. People there think we are terrorists, visas are very difficult. And why is this? It is our leaders who do not understand that we can only grow by looking out, not by making our country an island."

*

In the centre of Shiraz is the tomb of Hafiz. Born in Shiraz around 1320, Hafiz is a celebrated poet throughout the Farsi-speaking world. His work is also said to have mystical qualities, so that if one seeks guidance on a particular question, by opening a book of his poetry and pointing at random, the answer will be revealed in the lines. It was dusk when the gates to the tomb opened, and the plants of the garden were letting out that breath of moisture, which comes when the heat of the sun recedes. Long shallow pools of water, lined with light blue tiles reflected the outdoor lights of the courtyard garden. Above the hushed sounds of the visitors, the loudspeakers played gentle musical arrangements of Hafiz's poems. In the centre an octagonal sandstone cupola arched over his gravestone, which lay flat like a tabletop, inscribed with a verse of his poetry. A smiling man offered us Ramadan sweets from a box lying open on the stone. Many of the visitors were young and walked in mixed groups. They carried books of his poetry, which they read aloud to each another as they circled the courtyard. One group fell into step with us. They only knew French, did we? For an hour they translated poems from the Farsi to French.

> "Into the mirror of my cup
> the reflection of your glorious face fell
> And from the gentle laughter of love,
> into a drunken state of longing I fell
>
> Struck with wonder by the beauty of the picture
> that within my cup I beheld
> The picture of this world of illusion

from the reflection of my mind fell

Beneath the sword of grief of love for you
there lies a joy no tongue can tell
For that one who was slain by you
found happiness the instant the axe fell

From the house of prayer
into the house of drink I fell not of myself
From eternity it was meant to be,
you came to me and into drunkenness I fell[15]"

Yet how alien was the Iran of Hafiz to those living in the Iran of the Ayatollah. He used the language of intoxication and spoke of love and yearning for his muse, Shakh-e Nabat, a woman who was not his wife. In modern Iran, wine and women were both forbidden, hidden, illicit.

We became used to the five minute introductory remarks about the state of the country, often made in an apologetic slightly embarrassed way: from Iraj in military service, covering the military insignia on his arms "because when we are with the army it is illegal for us to talk to foreigners," and asking us for advice on emigration: from Mohammed whom we met in the bus stop, his scars still fresh from the twenty lashes he received for drinking alcohol, and of course from Raza Khan with his Harvard concepts and buzzwords.

*

---

[15] "Into the Mirror of My Cup," Hafiz, trans. Newell, J. R. 2001

In Bam, we found ourselves back on a more established travellers' route. The courtyard of the Akbar guesthouse had a familiar mixed bag of international backpackers. Two Japanese boys sat wrapped up in their Afghan blankets, which they had bought in a whistle-stop tour through Afghanistan the week before. They had travelled through Kabul, Bamyam, Mazar-i-Sharif, and back to Peshawar before making their way to Iran across the southern border. "At night we hear bombs and shooting, and we see someone shot."

I asked them about Bamyam, where famously the Taliban had destroyed the huge cliff-carved Buddhas. They replied, "In Bamyam there is now only a hole. A hole shaped like the Buddha..." They would shortly depart for Baghdad, the next stop on a daredevil itinerary of the world's hotspots. Dangerous places seemed to have a strange allure to Japanese students, or perhaps because Japan was less involved in the recent conflict they were less at risk.

There was a group of fifteen "over-landers" who arrived in what looked like an armoured bus. It was a funny mixture of nationalities and ages who gently squabbled and flirted among themselves. The driver was a Turkish South Londoner and the tour leader was his girlfriend, a pale Dutch girl. Every evening in the guesthouse courtyard they held a group discussion on what route the armoured bus should go on next, which invariably ended up in arguments and snide back-biting.

It was a relief to sit and chat in the courtyard, puffing on the water pipe that Iranians call the quelion and listening to the guesthouse owner's son, Master Akbar's jokes about Turks, the butts of Iranian humour. At seven o'clock he served the assembled guests with the home cooking of his mother, who remained invisible in the back room of the house. A favourite was the Khoresht bademjun: aubergines cooked in oil with onions and garlic and spiced with turmeric and cardamom. The mixture was mashed to a chunky puree and covered in a layer of yoghurt, thick with parsley and other chopped herbs. It was garnished with saffron. We ate it straight from the dish, scooped up with lavash bread.

Master Akbar brought out refilled bowls for the water pipes and endless glasses of sweet black tea. He continued to regale the combined audiences with increasingly obscure and obscene jokes breaking into hysterical giggles even before he had reached the punch line. His friend, Abbas, came to visit and they made fun of each other – a well rehearsed double act. "Abbas, Abbas do not listen to him, his father is a Turkish donkeyman."

"Ha no. This Master Akbar he belly-dances for money…"

We stayed up late in the warm night, lounging on the cushions and sampling different flavours of tobacco until Mr Akbar shouted at his son that he was keeping the neighbours awake so we would all have to go to bed.

The reason for coming so far East to Bam was for Simon to photograph the Arg e Bam, the mud brick village and citadel abandoned in the nineteenth century when the Afghans invaded the area which was now being painstakingly restored with mud bricks, hand-made like the originals. It was a warren of crumbling arches, doorways, and fallen-in roofs with colours and shadows that changed from the flat brightness of the midday light, through to the rich orange and long shadows of the evening. When we climbed up to the citadel and looked down on the tumbling village it had an abstract beauty, the rhythmic black lines of doorways against a uniform chalky red. It reminded me of Anthony Gormley's massive public art works; rooms of simple clay figures each staring with a pair of black eyes. There were no more than a dozen visitors to the massive site, and they added to the eerie experience of the abandoned city, gliding down forgotten alleys, past doorways as dark as their chadors. On the highest point was the governor's house, commanding views over the surrounding country. We could see the rich green of Bam's date plantations and the abrupt change where the desert started, a flat dust-pan all the way to the purple hills in the North, and the flat horizon of the East where the invaders of this abandoned city once came from.

CHAPTER 12

Chak Chak

"Zoroastrians are not fire worshippers,"[16] Massoud told us as we drove out of Yazd. "They believe that the earth, the air, the water and fire are all holy elements. The reason people think they are fire worshippers is because it says in their holy book that they must pray towards the light, so they are often praying in front of candles or flames." Massoud was a student in Yazd and had offered to skip his classes for a day to take us to the Zoroastrian holy mountain, "Chak-Chak," our fourth holy mountain. "Here in Yazd is the centre of the Zoroastrian religion and there are maybe 40,000 Zoroastrians around Yazd." Massoud wore baggy jeans and trainers. His hair was long and carefully dishevilled unlike most Iranian men who sport the classic bouffant (short at the sides and long on top,

---

[16] Zoroastrianism is based on the ideas of Zoroaster who is thought to have lived in North Eastern Iran around 1200 BC. He claimed to have been taught personally by God (Ahura Mazda) in a series of visions, and emphasis on personal responsibility is a hallmark of Zoroastrianism. He called for the worship of Ahura Mazda and rejected the lesser gods of the incumbent religion. By the 6th century BC Zoroastrianism had become the official state religion of Persia.

It was replaced with Islam after the defeat of Yazdgard III by the Arabs in 635 but continued as a minority faith. Today there are an estimated 40,000-90,000 Zoroastrians in Iran, 90,000 in India known as Parsis, mostly in and around Bombay and 25,000 in Europe, principally the UK, with a similar number in the US.

immaculately brushed back in a light wave (I was also given this treatment when I went for a haircut in Iran.) He was a Muslim, but having grown up in Yazd, he knew all about the Zoroastrians and assured us he would be an excellent guide.

On the way to the Zoroastrian mountain shrine we stopped at the Towers of Silence, the Zoroastrian burial towers. These two short conical structures sit on mountains overlooking Yazd. "The Zoroastrians believe the earth and fire are holy so they cannot use them to get rid of dead bodies. They cannot burn or bury the dead. What they do is leave the bodies in the tower and let the vultures come down and eat the meat. When there is only a skeleton left the priest pushes it into the stone pit in the middle and breaks it up with a long stick." There are two towers outside Yazd; a new one was built on a neighbouring peak, when the hole in the first filled up with bones. Thirty years ago it was decided in Iran that this method of disposal was a health risk (the vultures would sometimes drop body parts in the surrounding area) and Iranian Zoroastrians are now buried in the ground in a concrete lined grave. The buildings felt sinister and industrial; the wide walls reminded me of factory cooling towers, and cut out the wind so that it suddenly felt still and quiet inside. The pit in the centre was now filled in with stones, which had settled leaving a metre of emptiness as the old bones turned to dust.

We drove across the desert, away from Yazd, leaving the towers behind us. The road was unbending on the featureless desert, which stretched for plantless miles into a horizon of airborne dust. Mountains erupted from the flats, barren and harsh-looking with impregnable cliffs and rocks that would already be burning hot. They rose like dark islands, their ridges irregularly serrated and ending as abruptly as they began. I dozed in the heat, and woke up when the desert ran across the road, the tarmac interrupted by the encroaching grit and pebbles of this possessive landscape.

*

Like other religious leaders, Zoroaster sought respite from the world and found spiritual enlightenment in the peace and isolation of mountains. He lived on Mount Asnavant (in modern Azerbaijan) for a number of years, practising solitary meditation and it was on this mountain that he is believed to have gained the power and energy to venture forth as a spiritual teacher. On Mount Ushi-darena (in the Mount Albroz range) Zoroaster was said to have attained illumination and received the knowledge of the supreme god, Ahura Mazda. Many Zoroastrian holy places came to be located on lonely mountains; indeed Herodotus wrote about the Zoroastrians in the fifth century BC and noted. "It is not their custom to make and set up statues and temples and altars…but…they offer sacrifices on the highest peaks and mountains." Originally these would have been nothing more than holy rocks or springs, possibly places of pagan veneration that were gradually absorbed by the Zoroastrians and developed with simple buildings and temples (syncretism a feature of this ancient religion just as it would be with Christianity, Buddhism and Islam). In other parts of the country these old holy sites have been forgotten or absorbed into the Islamic tradition – layers of absorption on top of each other - but around Yazd, six of these mountain shrine sites survive, each still celebrating its annual Pir or festival.

From a distance there was nothing impressive about the mountain of Chak-Chak. It rises from the desert floor, just like the other rocky islands, no taller or shapelier than its neighbours. It was only when we got closer that we could see what set it apart. Half way up the mountain, hidden from the road by a cliff-covered spur was an incongruous splash of green, formed by a cluster of vegetation around a spring, a tiny oasis in this unforgiving dryness. Below the trees a series of modern buildings had been built, in Mediterranean white and pale blue. These were added thirty five years ago when it was decided more effective provision should be made for the large numbers of visitors to the shrine who had been camping in tents on the desert floor.

"Normally, the Zoroastrian pilgrims walk from here," Massoud told us. "At the first sight they have of the temple, they leave their cars and buses and walk." But in the baking early afternoon sun we preferred to drive. We left the car at the bottom of the hill and climbed up the twisting path that turned to steps as the mountain steepened. After ten minutes climbing we were among the buildings, set on neat concrete terraces, doorless and empty. "At the Pir this is full of pilgrims. So many, you cannot move and people have to sleep on the terraces and pathways. Always singing, dancing, cooking, eating." But now, out of season, it was empty and the only sounds we made were echoed back to us by the mountain wall. The Pir is from 14-18 June and as many as 10,000 Zoroastrian pilgrims attend the site as part of the circuit of the six main sites around Yazd. Nowadays they arrive in a convoy of buses and taxis, but a man from Sharifbad, Agha Rustam, remembered the pilgrimage in the days before motor vehicles.

"Then it was a full 24 hour journey to the shrine from the most southerly village and even the Sharifabadis used to travel all through the night. They sent an advance party the night before with donkeys laden with food and bedding… the main band of pilgrims would set off in the cool of the evening, heading straight across the desert. If the night were dark, the leader of the caravan sometimes played the surna, [Persian oboe] to keep them together, and occasionally lit a flare-fire along the way."[17]

Above the new buildings was the Zoroastrian chapel, where the solitary khadem (care taker) appeared to open the brass doors, embossed with Achaemenid guards, each bearing a dart, imitations of which we had seen at Persepolis in Shiraz the week before. We were given little white hats to wear inside the chapel, which covered all our hair and looked like the hygiene hats that butchers wear. Three flames burned in a metal lamp in an alcove cut into the cave wall and above us, through railings, we could see the cool greenery that surrounded the dripping spring, which gives the site its onomatopoeic name, "Chak-Chak". A large willow tree grew through a purpose-built hole in the roof of the chapel, its lower branches covered in the same fabric knots we had seen around holy sites in Kyrgyzstan – more wishes by the faithful.

We sat gazing at the flame while Massoud told us the legend of the holy spring, set during the Arab invasion of the Persian Empire in 635. The Arab army took the Persian capital of Cresiphon and continued pushing east in pursuit of Emperor Yazdegard III and his family. When they drew close, Yazdegard's daughter Hayat-Banu fled into the desert alone on her horse. For miles she galloped across the dusty expanse until her horse tired and could go no further. She left the worn out animal in the desert and continued on foot, the Arab soldiers still in hot pursuit and growing ever larger on the

---

[17] The experience of Agha Rustam related in "A Persian Stronghold of Zoroastrianism," Mary Boyce. Oxford Press, 1977.

horizon. In front of her was this barren cliff face and there was nothing to do but climb it. But the rocks were sharp and the cliff was steep so that her legs ached and she could go no further. Exhausted, alone and frightened she lay down and cried. She prayed to the Zoroastrian god, Ahura Mazda, to protect her from the approaching Arabs and she surrendered herself to his hands. By this time the Arabs were at the base of the mountain and had started to climb towards her, their curved swords drawn and ferocious grins on their faces, now they had their quarry cornered. With renewed fear Hayat Banu got up to run away but she could not move her willow cane, which had become stuck in a cleft of the rock. The cleft widened as she tugged the stick and then opened to allow her into a cavern in the mountain where she was perfectly concealed. The Arabs were maddened, she had been surrounded, how had she outwitted them? They cursed her as they searched all over the mountain but she remained hidden in the cleft of rock by the grace of Ahura Mazda.

The rescue of the Persian princess was not the only miracle that took place that day. Where her tears had fallen on the barren rock a spring began to drip, with the same sound that her tears first made and her cane remained stuck in the rock and sprouted into a willow tree, which continued to be watered by the new spring. To this day the tree is called "Old Stick," and can make pilgrims' wishes come true when they tie a knotted cloth to it. The tree has a blackened appearance, which is said to be because of the legend that the tree catches fire and renews itself, phoenix-like, every thousand years, but is more likely to be caused by soot from the perpetual flame. Massoud pointed down at the runnel of water from the stream, lined with dark green maidenhair fern. "They say that that is her hair running out of the mountain where she is hidden away and safe."

Hayat-Banu was not the only daughter to escape the Arabs. Her sister was also swallowed into the rock of a mountain, now another holy place where the Banu-Pirs (near Sharifbad) is celebrated. The Seti-Pir is celebrated where her mother was swallowed into yet another mountain, with two of her attendants. The Arabs won a decisive victory at the battle of Al Qadisiyah in 635 over the army of Yazdegard III, who fled and was eventually killed in 652 by one of his own people. The English academic, Mary Boyce has suggested that these legends of women being absorbed into mountains are probably based on a very similar Muslim legend connected with the city of Ray south of Tehran, but she adds that,

"The tale of his [Yazdegard's] daughters' sufferings embodied both the communities' sorrow for the fate of their kings, and their own sadness as a persecuted minority…Moreover, according to the legend, Ahura Mazda intervened in his mercy to save the princess…there was thus faith and hope in the legend also…"[18] In some ways I found it a rather sinister story. It wasn't really an escape, the mountain didn't temporarily conceal her it simply swallowed her up, and still holds her, just letting her hair flow out in the stream. But as Boyce pointed out, as a religious story it struck just the right notes; the Persians did not win but still a martyr was born.

Until the Arab invasion the most important Zoroastrian religious centre had been further west near Shiraz at Naqsh-e Rostam where the Persian Kings were buried in rock-carved tombs watched over by engravings of the winged-ring symbol of Ahura Mazda. The transfer of devotion to Chak-Chak was due to the geographical location of the remaining Zoroastrians

---

[18] Ibid.

- pushed east as the Arab armies overran Persia. But it also symbolised the entrenched position of Zoroastrianism; reduced from state religion to a threatened minority religion in the face of a Muslim onslaught. No longer was their holy place a gloriously carved cliff face. Now it had become a tiny mountain-side shrine, isolated and protected by cliffs. The swallowing up of the Emperor's daughters represented the new introversion of the Zoroastrian minority. Its glory days were over.

The khadem sat nodding as we listened to the story then wordlessly led us down to the terrace where Massoud set up the stove for a late lunch in one of the simple kitchen rooms that are on the end of each terrace. As we passed a row of trees watered from the spring above, Massoud told us what each of them were, "Myrtle, Pomegranate, Fig, Cyprus…" A miniature arboretum high on the barren cliff. There were still ashes in the hearth from the previous Pir and we cleared them away then chopped onions and poured them into the steaming pot at Massoud's instructions. Eggs and tomatoes followed to make a delicious soup served with crisp, salty, thick barbari bread. The khadem brought us water in a battered tin pot, and told us,

"No need to boil it, it is safe to drink now. It is from the spring…"

*

The taxi driver was asleep in the back of his car and looked grumpy when Massoud threw pebbles at the roof to wake him up. We drove back through the desiccated desert, revived by our meal while Massoud leaned round from the front seat. "You have whisky in Scotland. I know the names of very good whisky. J&B, Johnnie Walker..." He told us about his whisky sessions with friends, the driver nodding with relish when he recognised the brand names. "Iranian wine is excellent too," he told us, "if you know the right person to buy it from. I can buy it for you if you like." We declined the offer, it would only be a couple of weeks until we would be free to indulge in Turkey without risking corporal punishment. I asked Massoud what the exact punishment was for drinking.

"Well you would probably be let off and only warned because you are a foreigner."

"But if we *weren't* foreigners."

"Well they might let you off because you are young."

"No, but if they were to punish us, what would it be?"

"They might not even catch you..."

"Yes, ok. But if they did."

He paused for a few seconds recollecting the punishment. "If it is the first time and only drinking, nothing else. No fighting or damaging, then it is maybe twenty lashes, but maybe as many as eighty. But the wine is *delicious* – it is worth eighty lashes. In Shiraz there is a place where you can buy. You go into the shop, it is a food shop, and you leave your bag on the floor. You ask for special Pepsi, one bottle, two bottles, whatever you want. Then you pay maybe 2,000 tomans (£1.50) for one litre. You go away and come back to pick up your bag and it will have the wine in it. It is very safe, you would not get caught."

The conversation moved on to Ramadan. It had been an easy day today, as travelling meant we were all allowed to eat. There had been none of the hasty munching of bananas and biscuits in quiet back alleys that we had resorted to when sightseeing in the towns. Massoud told us about his first Ramadan. "I was ten and it was so difficult. It was in the middle of the summer so it was very hot - I had gone swimming in the day but I had to be careful not to let the water cover my head because in the Koran if your head is all in water it means you have broken your fast. I wanted to cool my head in the water but to do this I had to get out of the pool and splash water on my hair and face. That is allowed." Although he was allowed to break his fast today, because of our travel, he would have a day's fasting after Ramadan to make up for the one day he had missed.

"It is an important time of the year and I will always do it. It is good for the body and the digestion. For one month it is rested and helps us to not get fat." I doubted how good it was for the body. A fellow passenger on one of our bus journeys told me about military service during Ramadan, when daylong exercises were undertaken in the mountains without food or water. Men collapsed and became delirious.

"But that is wrong," Massoud countered, "our rules tell us that if we are playing sport, or at war, or if we are ill or pregnant, or travelling then we must not fast. Ramadan will never do anyone harm, only to people who are not educated and do not know the laws."

We drove on to Meybod, an ancient stop for the desert-crossing caravans. The gatekeeper was tracked down and we were let into the caravanserai where arched sleeping platforms looked onto a sunken covered pool fed by the gently sloping qanats (underground water channels) which transported cool water from distant springs. Nearby was the ice house, an egg-shaped room half above ground and half below, flanked by two wind towers that caught any breeze in the air and channelled it across pools of water to keep the building as cool as possible.

Massoud was still talking. He had moved onto the subject of his marriage. "Well, I know who I will marry," he said with solemn certainty. "Because it is the sister of my best friend. He does not know yet although he is a very good friend. I know I will marry her because I love her. Soon I will talk to my parents and they will talk to hers, and then we will get married. Even though it is a love marriage, it is important our parents are involved." He was terribly serious as he said it. We joked about what his best friend's reaction would be to this but it seemed to be a cause for genuine concern so we kept off the topic. Had he talked to her?

"No."

"Do you think she will marry you?"

"Yes, I think she will." There was little hesitation. "I have looked at her and she has looked back at me so that I know she loves me too. I need to tell my friend and then my parents… there is no one else I can marry."

The desert was now less harsh in the evening light. As we drove back Massoud sang to us over the noise of the engine. First, he sang of an exiled Iranian who had fled the revolution to Turkey but now missed his homeland. Then, he sang Hafiz set to music. Like so many other young Iranians we met, Massoud was a complex, uncategorizable mixture of tradition and modernity, some parts of his religion critical to his self image, others already discarded. He was the same age as me and I imagine I would have been similar to Massoud if I were an Iranian student. Part of me would react against intrusive rules from the state that acted like a domineering parent, and it was no surprise to find how bitter Massoud felt towards the restrictions this placed on his twenty-four year-old life. The feeling that I had not expected but absolutely understood now

I was here, was Massoud's reaction against western secularity. He took pride in both the history of his nation and a strong muslim self-image. His devotion was to a culture that was not reflected in the Ayatollah's regime but he also rejected Western secularity. However, in the country in which he lived, this blend of proud, liberal Islam and secular ideas had to remain something guiltily private.

Massoud's voice soared above the motor, the Farsi elegant and slow. When he stopped he explained to us, "It is a song about a man who loves so much that he feels he is drunk with wine."

*

Simon wanted to photograph the mosques of Isfahan in the dawn light so it was still dark when he threw his pillow across the room at my sleeping head. "Late already. Got to catch the early light." We stumbled through cold streets, yawning and breakfastless, until we got to Emam Khomenei square, now washed in pink light. We walked the length of the square with the quiet sounds of morning: the flap of pigeons' wings, the rattle of metal shutters going up, the swish of a brush against paving stones.

The entrance point at the north iwan of the Emam Mosque twists away from the square so that the mosque is angled to point towards Mecca. The inner courtyard is open to the sky and the low-angled sun set a-glitter the acres of mosaic. Yellow and turquoise arabesques swirled symmetrically, interwoven on an indigo background. The sections of mosaic were arranged in rectangular blocks traced with arch shapes, echoing the larger arches that gave onto the iwans on either side. Pure white-on-blue tiles of looping Persian script ran in strips around the courtyard, the writing so stylised that the letters became indistinguishable from the abstracted flowers above and below it. The water in the central ablutions pool was still, reflecting the arches and pillars that surrounded it.

We lay on our backs beneath the dome of the main sanctuary and gazed at the intricacies of the semi-sphere of tiling. This cupola, like the rest of the mosque, was on a spectacularly grand scale. In the dimness of this inner sanctuary Simon held his camera stock-still and released a two second exposure to capture the cupola design. In the centre of the floor there was a hard black stone, distinct from the sandstone surroundings. When I tapped this stone with my foot, echoes bounced around the sanctuary, twelve distinct echoes (although scientists have counted forty nine.)

Two overalled men appeared from the gloom at the far end of the sanctuary, their beckoning fingers pointing down as is the Iranian way. They huddled round us conspiratorially, casting nervous glances over their shoulders, and pointed to a wooden door. "Go up, go up?" A staircase, then wooden ladders led up to the roof where they instructed us to keep close to the walls because if the imams saw us – they drew hands across their throats (I wasn't sure if this would be their fate for taking us up or ours for coming up.) These men were working on the restoration of the dome. The tiles have to be replaced periodically and they explained that this was because of the acid from pigeon excrement which erodes and discolours the exterior tiles. Rather than working on scaffolding all day, a section of the dome tiling is constructed on the ground by laying the mosaic face down on a wooden mould shaped like a skateboarding ramp. This is then lifted onto the roof with a derrick and attached to the bare strip, like peeling an orange in reverse.

They pointed to the minaret with questioning eyes and wrote down the small sum they wanted to take us up. I looked at the towering turquoise column, the designs on it in squares and diamonds rather than swirling floral patterns of the dome. I was nervous about it; if the immams would disapprove of us being on the roof what would they do if they saw us up one of their minarets? But Simon had decided already that he had to have a bird's eye view.

The minaret's internal staircase began reasonably wide but towards the top it was so narrow that I had to turn my shoulders sideways. It was claustrophobic and dark. At last a trapdoor opened onto a narrow ledge that ran around the top of the minaret. They told us to keep low, below the wooden lattice that surrounds the ledge. Through the criss-cross of wood I could see a dusty-brown Isfahan stretched out before me. Far to the south-west was the curve of the Zayandeh river and its eleven multi-arched bridges. Beneath me lay the expanse of the square, rectangles of grass, fountains, the pillars of the Ali Qapu Palace on one side and the pink-ochre cupola of the Lotfalla mosque on the other.

Simon held his camera one handed above the lattice and snapped away one-handed. "Spectacular, spectacular. Glad we got up early. Told you it would be worth it."

*

We flew across country from Isfahan to Tabriz where it was noticeably colder; we were higher here and further north. I sat in the draughty hotel dining room and wrote lists of people I still had to send postcards to, while the doormen huddled round a diesel stove in the corner. There suddenly didn't seem much time left on the trip. Only one more Iranian city to go, and only one more holy mountain. Now we were nearing the end I wanted to draw the time out. I was fond of waking up in new accommodations every few days, of pausing when we wanted to but always having somewhere to go. I had reached a kind of equilibrium where constant movement and change was the familiar routine and I couldn't see myself stopping.

We prowled the dark streets of Tabriz looking for somewhere warm and found an institutional-looking tea-house, with white-topped formica tables running the length of the room in two parallel rows. Toothless men sat chewing sugar cubes and slurping tea in between lungfuls of smoke from large quelions. We ordered tea and one of the monstrous quelions, but found the smoke far too harsh. It was not the flavoured tobacco we had become used to, but a rough, dry, pure tobacco. We put the pipe to one side and drank our tea without speaking, watching the men mumbling to one another as they sat in their tea-house lines, trying to absorb an atmosphere that we would soon leave behind.

*

Nasser Khan proudly announced that he could speak eight languages. He was a state employee at the tourist information centre, but since the troubles in Afghanistan the tourists in Tabriz were few and far between. "One or two people come every two days." Because of this drastic reduction in numbers his tourist service was completely personalised. All morning he walked with us round the labyrinthine market clearly enjoying the attention of being a well-known face about town. When he was greeted by the shopkeepers his smile curved down, as if he was slightly bashful about the attention, "you know this is what happens when you are a little bit famous around the town."

He was light skinned and ginger, although he assured us he was a genuine Tabrizi who simply happened to be rather distinguished looking.

Men drank tea from tulip shaped glasses in the gloom of curtained off carpet shops which were a guilty haven from the abstinence of Ramadan. When we entered they brought us tea and showed us down to the bowels of the shop where they laid out lines of carpets under bare light bulbs. Killims, alive with the tribal motifs of nomadic life lay in the shape of crosses - originally the edges would have been sewn up in boxes to transport the children and household items on the backs of donkeys or camels. The strings of tassels used to decorate the central tent pole hung around the door and the hot-water-bottle-shaped carpet bags used to carry salt lay in dusty stacks against the wall. The carpets in this shop were rough and irregular, quite different from the intricate Persian designs of the silk carpets that we had seen in the tourist shops of Isfahan. The material here was camel or goat wool and the carpets still smelt of lanolin. We wandered from shop to shop, where, behind drapes, Ramadan was studiously ignored, and overburdened ourselves with souvenirs.

CHAPTER 13

Ararat

Sixty miles from the Turkish border I saw a snow-capped peak, an apparition, a sheet-draped ghost above the dust-mist of a dry horizon. Surely it could not be the Turkish mountains so soon? We still had two hours of driving to go before we hit the border. The shape became clearer, and it could be nothing else but Ararat, its volcanic bulk sharply etched against the clear sky; the snow like hardened rivulets of water-icing running down its snub nose: our fifth and final holy mountain. A smooth curve to the East connected it to Little Ararat, its sister mountain over a thousand metres lower, snowless and made of matt black volcanic rock from the domed top all the way down to the valley like a crumpled hijab veil. The drab surrounding hills seemed just ruffles on the landscape alongside these twin peaks.

There was a long queue at the Turkish border post, full of Iranian traders and their heaped-up packages of sweets, cigarettes, and sacks of vegetables. As non-commercial traffic, we were allowed to bypass this queue, and were shepherded into a fenced gateway leading to Turkish customs. Our passports were passed to the front and we followed more slowly, climbing over bales of parsley and bursting a newspaper parcel of garlic. The unfortunate Iranian garlic importer stuffed the escaped garlic bulbs into the pockets of his coat, and when they were full he crammed them down the front of his shirt, the odd clove escaping between the buttons. The Turkish side of the border was a building site, the customs house a portacabin and the bank where I bought visa stamps was hidden behind piles of twisted reinforced concrete.

Ararat towered over us as we drove to the frontier town of Dogubayazit, dominating the skyline. I could see its full height, a limited palette of colours on its lower slopes, patches of umber and charcoal grey that coalesced up the flanks and were obscured near the top by a veil of snow.

This corner of Turkey is a sensitive border zone lying next to Armenia, Iran and Azerbaijan. It is also the heartland of the PKK; a Marxist-Leninist Kurdish paramilitary group, which began carrying out attacks in 1984 and has apparently left over 28,000 dead over a ten-year campaign. The retaliatory attacks and counter-strikes by the Turkish military were extremely bloody and instability put this part of Turkey off-limits to tourists until 2000. A cease-fire was agreed in 2000 when the PKK leader Abdullah Ocalan was captured in Kenya and began demanding a strategy of peaceful negotiation from his cell in Turkey. Despite the improved security situation there is still a strong military presence and groups of uniformed soldiers loitered on street corners and in the cafes. Bulky Turkish army boys with marine hair-styles threw sugar cubes at us while we breakfasted in the local teahouse, a habit we tolerated - I imagine it got quite boring for them over here on the edge of their country and it was best not to make a fuss when two against twenty.

Dogubayazit had the familiar border-town feeling of impermanence. But with the vulnerability of the frontier come economic opportunities; there was money to be made on this border. The main square was alive with trucks coming and going with piles of killims and carpets. In the vegetable market the Iranian wholesalers' loaded vans headed further west into Turkey. Goods went east too; lines of trucks waited at checkpoints on the road outside Dogubayazit, to be searched and checked by the army before they were allowed to continue to the border.

It was obvious which side of the border we were on. Signs outside shops announced, "Tuborg… Carlsberg," and the cafés stayed open all day despite it still being Ramadam. There were postcards in the shops of pouting girls in swimsuits and on the street the women wore coloured headscarves tied in knots at the back of their heads, which looked strangely messy after the uniform plain black hijab of Iran. Music shops blared pirated copies of the latest Turkish and Kurdish discs through speakers on the pavements.

Melik was a soldier but he did not look like one. He had a narrow frame and his hair was longer than the standard crew cut. "When you go for your military service, they send you to places far away from your home. I am from Ankara so they send me here."

"It must be tough to be away for so long in these parts."

"It has been a long time. I have now four months left, and I have done fourteen already. I am not allowed to go home very much. It is difficult, but it is not so hard for me. I do not have to go on patrol; I do not go in a tank. I am a DJ."

"What, for parties?"

"No, no, a DJ on the radio. We operate a radio station, speaking to the Kurds around here, trying to promote peace. It is all very well to have tanks on their doorstep and shoot them if they try and attack, but it is better that they do not want to attack, no?" He had been dreading his military service, and had managed to put it off for six years by postponing the completion of his philosophy degree from Ankara University, and taking a Master's degree straight afterwards. But finally there was no excuse for him and he was sent to the military training centre where he had performed very badly, "I am not really a physical person." However, as an educated, older than average entrant who had a way with words, he was sent east and given work on the military radio station.

"We play music that they like, not Kurdish music, but modern music that they want to listen to, and then every half hour I read out a statement that tells them not to raise arms, or that the central government cares about them, or that Abdullah Ocalan wants them to be peaceful. I think it is a good system. And it is good for me too, I would hate to be patrolling this place like these other soldiers. But I was still very scared of coming here. When I was living in Ankara all through the 1990s there were problems here; many, many deaths, of soldiers and of the normal people living here. I have Kurdish friends in Ankara and they tell me that the people here are in danger from the army who think they are PKK and from the PKK who think they are not agreeing with their politics. It was a very sad place to live. So, I am scared to come out here; for me it was like a different country. But things are more peaceful now. I was thinking I would be in a barracks all the time with bombs flying, but no. I can sit in a teahouse. It is fine."

*

As Marco Polo passed through this part of the country he related, "You must know that it is in this country of Armenia that the Ark of Noah exists on top of a certain great mountain on the summit of which snow is so constant that no one can ascend."[19] Of all the places to leave an Ark none could be more impressive than Ararat. The name reminded me of the most exciting Sunday school story of them all and an illustrated book that had fascinated me as a child. It showed a picture of God, a middle aged man with a tidy white beard in a brown dressing gown, creating a rainbow from his outstretched hands while an ark teetered on the point of a far peak.

According to the Old Testament, as the wickedness of man spread across the Earth God grew angry and decided to punish the world with a great flood. Only one good man, Noah, was chosen to survive this punishment along with seven companions. God instructed him to build an Ark and fill it with a pair of each of the animals on earth "of all flesh, both of fowl, and of cattle, and of every creeping thing that creepeth upon the earth." (Genesis 7,8). The flood came and covered the earth destroying all the people and animals apart from Noah, his companions and his animals. For 150 days the Ark sailed on the high waters and Noah sent out doves and ravens to try to find dry land. At last one of the doves returned with a leaf from an olive tree and Noah knew that the water was gradually subsiding. As the water drained away the high peaks of the mountains emerged like islands and the Ark came to rest on the highest of them all, Mount Ararat. God spoke to Noah, promising he would never destroy mankind again and sent a rainbow as a symbol of this promise.

The story of Nuh in the Koran has its origin in the Old Testament but the landing place of the Ark is less exact. It is described as landing on "Al Judi" which is the name of several hills in the Middle East but also means simply "the heights."

---

[19] "The Travels." Marco Polo, translated by Ronald Letham, Penguin, 1958.

"The Ark sailed along with them through waves towering like mountains... Thereafter, the command went forth: Swallow up thy water, O earth and O sky: Desist. The water subsided and the affair was closed. The Ark came to rest on Judi and the decree went forth; ruined are the wrongdoers." (Koran 11: 41-45)

The Judeo-Christian and Islamic account of the flood is in its turn based on a fund of Near-East traditions about floods of which the oldest surviving remnants are the cuneiform tablets[20] containing the Babylonian epic of Gilgamesh. It contains the story of Utnapishtim, the Babylonian Noah. Utnapishtim describes the flood:

"I entered the vessel and closed the door...

From the foundations of heaven a black cloud arose...

All that is bright turned to darkness...

The gods feared the flood,

They fled, they climbed into the heaven of Anu,"

Other Babylonian sources give the various names of the chief survivors as Xisuthros, Ubaratutu, and Khaistrata.

The legend of a great flood is not limited to the Near East. An Indian legend tells of Manu and his seven companions as the survivors of a great flood who were finally rescued when Vishnu in the form of a horned fish pulled their ship to Mount Himaret in the North Indian mountains. A legend of pre-Christian Ireland tells of Queen Ceseair and her court who sailed through a flood for seven and a half years. Indeed one is able to count over six hundred flood legends worldwide, reflecting a common fear and a common experience of freak natural conditions which are likely to have

---

[20] Found in the tablet library of King Ashurbanipal in the royal palace in Ninevah. "The Lost Ship of Noah." Charles Berlitz. W.H. Allen 1988.

taken place all over the world, caused by super-normal rainfall, the breaking of a river's banks, or tidal waves. The ravages of these one-off violent submersions were so extreme that the events entered the communal memory as legends, along with a human tale of isolated escape and survival.

Noah or Nuh is the most prominent of these because the story is related in the Bible and the Koran. However, there is something else compelling in the story that has prevented it from being written off as a myth. Firstly, the description of the building of the Ark is very precise. The measurements are given with great exactitude as 300 cubits by 50 cubits by 30 cubits as if this were a physical reality. Secondly, the Ark is pinned down in the Bible to landing in a particular place, Mount Ararat - a precise physical location that we can identify today. Ararat is also a location so inhospitable and difficult to explore, (covering 600 square miles, rising to over 5,000m and covered in glaciers) that it would be difficult to ever categorically deny that something still rests there. The precision of the evidence and the mysteriousness of the mountain keep the modern day pilgrims or Ark hunters coming back to search every year.

Ark hunters have long been coming to Ararat. A Byzantine monk named Jacob of Medzpin,[21] who later became Bishop of Nisbis, longed to see the Ark and prayed to God that his wish be granted before he finally set off to climb Ararat. After a day climbing the rocky lower slopes, he was tormented by thirst and overcome with fatigue and he lay down to rest. When he awoke, he found a spring miraculously appeared near where he had rested. Later, he continued his

[21] His story is recorded in "The Mission of Friar William of Rubruck: His Journey to the Court of the Great Khan." Tr. Peter Jackson, Hakluyt Society, 1990.

climb but after each rest, he would find upon waking that he was once again at the point at which he had started, presumably carried down by angels. God finally granted his prayers and sent an angel to visit him. The angel told Jacob to cease his attempts to climb the forbidden mountain and gave him a piece of the Ark. The angel then informed Jacob that the Ark was forbidden to mankind until such time as God should choose to reveal it.

More recently, travellers have told tales of locals finding timber high on the sides of Ararat and a monastery in Ahara apparently collected these relics of the Ark and even had an icon made out of them (no evidence remains of this, as the monastery was destroyed by an earthquake in 1840.) With the advent of aerial photography a number of possible Ark sites were identified, including the most commonly accepted one today which was later examined by a team led by David Fasold who used ultrasound, metal detectors and excavation to attempt to uncover evidence in the boat shaped mound. However, doubt still remains about this and every Ark site, and hunters continue to flock to Dogubayazit each year to trawl Ararat and the surrounding mountains for clues.

We had not been long in the Turkish border town of Dogubayazit when we met our first genuine Ark Hunter. By coincidence, he was from my uncle's hometown of Stornoway on the Isle of Lewis, where I had spent many wet summer holidays. He had been in the area for a couple of months and although he'd had no success so far, he was convinced his faith would bring him to it soon. "I don't know really what I'm looking for, but I will know when I find it. It could just be a wee bit of rock or wood, but it will be obvious to me when I see it."

He did not climb on the Sabbath and was unable to explore the mountain for the next week because of a terrible cold he had caught on the mountain on his last foray, which left him racking his lungs mid-sentence. "It's not so tough up there. I mean I'm not interested in getting to the top…" he paused while he cleared his throat and spat unceremoniously behind him, "I'm not interested in that, but last time I was up there I was just drawn upwards and there was maybe only one hundred feet to go. But it was awful icy and it was getting dark and you can't look for the Ark in the dark. I'm here to *look* not to climb. I'll leave the climbing to you." He added with a nod that could either have been disdainful or reserved Hebridean friendliness. His assessment of our journey reminded me of what the Indians had said to me at Kailash, "for you this is mountaineering, for us it is pilgrimage," the automatic disdain that tourists feel for other tourists whom they consider beneath them in motive or experience.

Donald climbed in a leather jacket and army surplus boots with no crampons, ice axe, or gloves. He had lost his tent and gas stove when shepherds stole his stash of equipment from under a rock on the mountain. After this catastrophe he had bought a double-barrelled shotgun from a Kurdish villager for £30, but "it's just for the wolves, like." His motorbike was stolen the previous week from Eli, the last village on the mountain, but when he reported this to the police they arrested him for climbing the mountain without permits. Permits can only be granted from Ankara, are expensive, and only last a week. He bribed the police $125 to avoid what he was told would be 3 months in prison. His trip seemed plagued by crises but with a Job-like resignation he tolerated them as though a series of painful trials just showed he was on the right route.

He had no time for the site now generally recognised to be the most likely, situated on the lower hills surrounding Ararat. "The Bible says that as the water receded gradually the other peaks became visible. That would be impossible unless the Ark landed on the highest point around." He pulled out a photocopied sheet of Genesis covered in annotations, highlights and scribbles and read from it, "Genesis chapter eight, verse four, 'And the Ark rested in the seventh month on the seventeenth day upon the mountains of Ararat.' Basically it became grounded on an underwater mountain. Then verse five, 'And the waters decreased continually until the tenth month: in the tenth month, on the first day of the month, were the *tops* of the mountains seen.' So when the Ark is grounded on a mountain there are *no* tops visible. It can't have been on any of the other hills round here because if the water was shallow enough for the Ark to ground itself on them, then the top of Ararat would have been visible already. D'you see what I mean?" He coughed loud and long, then added "It's an American theory," as if that was condemnation enough. "But it can only be on the mountain, up there," he looked up through the darkness to the moonlit slopes.

With so many hunters from both sides of the Atlantic, many generously funded by American evangelical groups, an incipient tourist industry has sprung up in Dogubayazit and Mehmet was the godfather of this industry. Within 5 minutes of our arrival in town, he was knocking on our hotel room door. "Hi, I'm Mehmet. You want to go to Iran, *no visa?*" His eyes flashed.

"Its OK, we've just come from Iran."

"We go to border then. You see refugees, smugglers... Taliban?" He changed tack. "You want to come and smoke opium. You'll be like this," he stretched his hands behind his head, closed his eyes and smiled. "Or hashish, cocaine?" Eventually his ambitions for our entertainment were scaled down to a one day tour of the official Ark site, with his warning that, at the price he was taking us for, his seven children would go hungry for a week (he was a consummate performer).

This site lies on the low hills opposite Ararat, half an hour from Dogubayazit on farm tracks. We drove past groups of heavily armed soldiers patrolling the border. One pair stopped our minibus and warned us not to take photos along the border. As we pulled away from them Mehmet shrugged: "Of course you can take photographs. I give you *my* permission..."

From a distance the official Ark site does look strikingly boat-shaped. Ridges of earth are raised like the ribs of an ancient hull and a mass of earth lies towards the stern like a great cabin. In his book "The Discovery of Noah's Ark" David Fasold meticulously explains the pieces of evidence; dimensions of the shape which match those in the Bible (if the Egyptian rather than the Hebrew cubit is used), drag-anchor stones in nearby villages, and regular traces of iron in the soil (that Fasold suggests are nails or pins). Most importantly, Fasold's excuse for the site not being on Ararat proper is that the direct translation of the passage which describes the landing place of the Ark in the Bible is *"the mountains of Ararat,"* (plural), although we already knew Donald's view on this. Fasold concludes, "Anyone who can't recognise this as a shipwreck either wouldn't know Noah's Ark if he was standing on it, or should have his theological cataracts removed..."

A newly constructed octagonal visitor centre overlooks the site, smelling of fresh paint. Inside, a series of photocopied articles and map tracings told the story of hoaxes and explorers, with the conclusion that in front of us was the genuine article. In the visitors' book the cynic and believer vied for space:

"Definitely a boat. Brought here to safe shores by the grace of God," J. Wilson from Texas.

"Is it real? It doesn't matter, it is our belief" scrawled a Korean visitor.

Simon was sceptical. "Mehmet, really this is a load of bollocks, isn't it? It's just earth." I think he had hoped to get a rise out of Mehmet by attacking the main artefact of Dogubayazit's tourist industry. Mehmet surprised him,

"Yes exactly, Mr Simon. It is very, very bollocks. They say the Ark is on this mountain – I take them. They are not allowed on that mountain so they say it is somewhere else – I take them. *I say* it is up there," he pointed to a nearby ridge of red rocks curved slightly like a mile long boat. "It is the biggest, no? For all the animals. I call it Mehmet's Ark…" He doubled over at his own joke. I imagine Mehmet agreed just as readily with a group of enthusiasts. Like the accomplished performer that he was, he told the audience exactly what they wanted to hear.

*

I had not expected to be able to climb Ararat. All the guidebooks told me that getting the necessary permit from Ankara was a lengthy and expensive process. It was also late November, which was not a month for climbing at altitude in this part of the world. However, for three days the sky had been clear and there had been no new snow on Ararat for several months. With Mehmet's encouragement we engaged a mountain guide. What a way to finish the trip, I thought, on Ararat, higher than any mountain in Europe. We were not sure of the legality of this, but thought the less we asked, the better. All Mehmet would say is that the policeman liked our guide very much. We would set off the next day, weather permitting.

Unfortunately, the weather did not permit. Great banks of cloud rolled in early in the morning and all day it drizzled in the streets of Dogubayazit. The bulk of Ararat that had dominated the skyline the day before was entirely obscured by a thick grey mist. We drank tea and the soldiers threw sugar cubes at us, while we hoped for better weather.

Mehmet visited us every day. He was bored too. It was the beginning of the slow winter season and he could see the last pay packet of our commission for the guide drifting away as the cloud hung on the mountain.

One evening, we went to a hotel on the hills above Dogubayazit where a Kurdish keyboard and vocal duo sang old favourites. We were joined by an American - another friend of Mehmet – who wore a beige waistcoat like a war photographer. He was an Ark hunter and had been to Ararat twenty-three times in the last twenty years on various hunts and surveys. His theories on the Ark were a strange mixture of hard, dry science and unquestioning belief in divine intervention. He also had an American fascination with conspiracy theory.

"The Turkish military know where it is, they've got evidence. That's for sure."

"Why are they keeping it to themselves?"

"Well, that's obvious. It would lead to all sorts of religious uprisings. This place is a real powder keg when it comes to things like that. The CIA have photographs of it too,

I know this because one man in my congregation back home told me that when he was a boy, his father (who was in the CIA) showed him a photograph of the Ark on the mountain, then burnt it in front of his eyes. The US government has proof of it, but they've got a deal going on with the Turkish government to keep this thing under wraps."

I asked him if he was planning a trip up the mountain.

"Well I can't really tell you about that. You know the situation with the military here…" I nodded knowingly. "All I know is I'll keep coming back here, until I do find it." This man, the last pilgrim I met, was from the richest country in the world but his devotion was no less strong and his motivation no more rational than any of the others. I carried on talking to him; listening to his theories on the hardiness of olive stones and what became of the dove that Noah sent out. He was a biblical literalist. "Garden of Eden? Yeah that's down in Syria – damn sure of that." It seemed that Ararat gave him the perfect ground to exercise his faith. Around Dogubayazit were shepherds and flocks and desert – a biblical landscape. There were soldiers impeding his search for the craft that had saved mankind (and they were not Christians.) A holy quest was meant to be testing, "Strait is the gate, and narrow is the way, which leadeth unto life," he preached, "and few there be that find it." At last Mehmet pulled me away and made me dance in a long line holding onto each other by our little fingers, gradually whirling round the room at a greater and greater speed.

When the clouds lifted after three days, it was only to reveal a great deal of fresh snow on the mountain. The scene had been completely transformed since our arrival in the heat a few days before. Winter had arrived in earnest and Ararat would not be climbable again until next year. Although I had not originally planned to finish the trip on the top of Ararat, the fact that for a few days it had been possible now made the impossibility seem like failure. Simon was more philosophical about the situation. He had developed a lasting aversion to altitude and Ararat was to be an exception to his own personal promise to himself never to go above 5,000m again in his life. "We can't go climbing so let's go to the beach."

We packed our bags and drove west the next morning, beginning a twenty-four-hour bus journey that would take us to the beaches of the Mediterranean and an international airport at Antalya. Muddy tundra stretched for miles on either side, interrupted by blisters of rocks. On the plains, flocks of sheep settled on patches of yellowed grass, the crouching figure of the shepherd occasionally distinct from the grey and brown sheep. Further on, the ground was higher and furrowed with the lines of ploughing. Snow lay in geometric lines, which converged into the distance to meet the grey sky. I looked back where Ararat should be, but the cloud had descended again, obscuring even the fresh snow of yesterday.

Epilogue

It was almost a year since I'd stopped work and started travelling. I'd spent the first few months of the new year writing, then I'd gone to Pakistan and India to satisfy the yearning that I'd felt as we met subcontinental traders and tourists in Tibet and Kashgar. Back home I remembered Ararat and the night we packed, thinking that the next day we would start climbing. I remembered Donald the ark hunter talking about seeing the summit a few hundred feet above him and that image of him in his army surplus jacket scanning the ground for wood and ignoring the summit lodged in my mind. "I'm here to search, not to climb, I'll leave that for you," he had said.

Flights to Turkey were cheap that year and because I was now free to do so I bought a last minute seat on a Thomas Cook charter flight to Bodrum. Bodrum is at the west end of Turkey, by the Meditteranean, ideally situated for the beaches and package resorts, but the wrong end for Ararat. We landed at midnight and most of the passengers were met by holiday reps and left in coaches to the coast, while I caught a taxi to the bus station in Antalya. The warm air blew through the taxi bringing with it the smell of pine forests and the sea. From Antalya I made the twenty-four-hour bus trip across Turkey for the second time.

The day passed in disjointed images as I slept, stared from the window and slept again. A beach resort, inflatable rings and animals hanging from shops by the road; apartment blocks that line city bypasses; thousands of balconies, each one a window onto another story; strings of washing, strewn toys, the film stills of assembled figures; a circle of black clad women preparing vegetables; a man staring hard at our bus while his son stares at him; evening, the martian vision of a red sun over the flat expanse of an inland lake, set in equally flat land; night time stops where I stumbled with a dry mouth to the strip-lit cafes, each roadside meal the same - oily meat and bread with tulip-shaped glasses of tea; then a milky dawn over the high land of east Turkey.

Mehmet's face crumpled with smiles when he remembered me from December. Of course he could fix me up with a guide, but I should know that prices had increased radically (of course they had). Then there was the additional cost of certain payments that had to be made because I still did not have permits. I cashed several travellers cheques and his smile broadened.

The guide was called Mustafa and he came from a family of nomads that lived on the slopes of Ararat. One hour from the road-head we reached their encampment; white tents, a shaded kitchen area and lazy yellow dogs dozing in the shelter of rocks. All the men were down working in Dogubayazit so it was an encampment of women and children. We drank straw-coloured tea made from herbs picked on the mountain, through sugar cubes held in our teeth. Mustafa passed around his mobile phone so that the women could talk to their men in the town. The matriarch of the family, hook-nosed and gap-toothed, smoked all the cigarettes her grandson passed to her and cackled down the phone (which she held in the unfamiliar way that my grandparents held mobile phones - awkward, amused, unsure how to listen and talk into such a short piece of plastic.)

We left the camp with a third member in our party, Mustafa's fourteen-year-old cousin, who was to make his first attempt on the summit. He was called Roshja and also wanted to be a mountain guide so that he could afford flash clothes and a mobile phone like Mustafa. He sang as he climbed, I don't know how.

It was a grinding, slow climb. We had started at around a thousand metres - four thousand metres to go in a steady slope that stretched all the way to the summit. The path wound in bends up the slope but still each step was up, relentlessly up. My pack was terribly heavy; I had been warned there was no water at camp one so I was carrying eight litres to last me for the two days until we reached camp II where there was snow to melt.

The dead weight of water swung from one shoulder to the other, a lazy pendulous motion, and the muscles in between my shoulders stiffened. When we rested in a series of stone enclosures, I asked Mustafa, "Camp One?" but he tutted and jerked his head up and to one side, that dismissive Asian gesture – of course not.

We climbed again as the sun weakened. In front of me Mustafa reached promontories and bluffs, several minutes before me, and I thought, surely that must be the camp. But each time he carried on moving steadily up, drawing away from me, pursued by the thin singing of Roshja's Kurdish laments.

At last, I saw their tiny figures, take off their sacks and hunch down to unpack. At last.

"Camp One?"

"No. Camp One and a half..." That explained it, I thought we had been climbing a very long time. "This is 3,700m. It is better. Camp One has no water. Here we have water." A stream splashed down the rocks nearby, fed by a tongue of snow a few hundred metres higher. I wished he had told me earlier. I had been carrying eight kilograms of water for nothing.

I put up the tent that Mehmet had hired to me. It turned out to be the kind of tent that one takes to a music festival – light plastic groundsheet and thin nylon walls, not really a piece of mountain equipment, but the evening was fair so it would not matter. As I cooked, Mustafa used his mobile phone to call a friend in town who relayed the weather forecast to him. Bad weather was coming he told me and if we were to have any hope of summiting we should try tomorrow rather than spending a night acclimatising at Camp II. I was dubious about going from one thousand metres to five thousand metres in two days but it looked like we didn't have a choice. I didn't fancy sitting out a storm in my flimsy plastic dome.

It was already light when the alarm went off at five in the morning. By six, we were climbing again, this time with the relief of having dumped my excess water. There was no vegetation above us; the ground was made of crumbling scree and dust. Higher up I could see huge black boulders of shiny obsidian glistening in the sun as if they were covered with water, but when I reached them they were dry and hot.

After an hour we reached camp II where Japanese faces peered at us from the double zipped doorways of expensive tents. We left most of our baggage here and continued up with light packs.

I could really feel the altitude now, I was panting and my heart racing, but the muscles in my legs still complained that not enough oxygen was being supplied. A headache had begun its gradual tightening behind my temples. I was feeling sick. The path was rougher and pebbles slid on stones beneath my boots, pulling me down. When we rested, I closed my eyes until Mustafa muttered under his breath, "Lessgo," and the pain would start again. Roshja had stopped singing.

After three hours of climbing we reached the snow. It was soft so there was no need for crampons. The wind had strengthened as we were climbing and above I could see clouds racing across the summit, gathering like circulating waves in the lee of the cone. I put on all my clothes but my cheeks were still exposed and bitten by the gusts. The final ridge flattened slightly then steepened for the summit. I rarely groan with exhaustion but on the final summit cone I exhaled and grunted with each step like an old man getting up from a low chair. We stumbled in wavering lines to the top, Roshja holding the straps of Mustafa's rucksack because he did not have an ice axe.

It's in climbing a mountain that one really appreciates just how huge and permanent it is; how much earth and rock and ice there is piled together, how tiny we are in comparison. But these mountains are not just physically immovable. The repeated element of syncretism – the absorption of holy mountains into one faith after another that was a feature of every holy mountain I visited – suggested that these mountains were spiritually immovable too. New religions could come and go but the mountains stayed holy. I had made this pilgrimage consciously without an allegiance to any one religion over another. I wanted my journey to be supra-religious. I was drawn by human devotion to these holy places rather than by my own devotion to any one religion. Now on the side of this huge mountain I fancied that these mountains were just the same; they simply overwhelmed. Now they happened to be Buddhist and Hindu and Muslim and Zoroastrian and Christian but before they had been Taoist and Bonnist and Shamanistic and Animist and Jewish and before that they were probably something else. Religions, like the pilgrims, would come and go while the holy mountains remained holy. One didn't need to be allied to a religion to feel the sense of awe.

I had imagined reaching the summit of Ararat many times. I'd been waiting to attempt it since Christmas and had visualised what I would do when I got there. I'd look east, into Armenia, Azerbaijan and Iran and then I'd look further to the horizon, where the Earth curves and disappears and I'd know that I was looking across the meandering string of holy mountains that we'd wandered between - thousands of pilgrim-miles across Asia. It would be a poetic moment; the climax of a year's travel, the symbolic end of a journey. On the top I would have my photo taken, ice axe aloft in a triumphant pose. We would shake hands and I would mutter some suitable words to my Kurdish guides.

None of this happened.

The summit crest was being buffeted by a gale that forced us to hold each other's shoulders and climb crab-like the last few metres to the iced-up top. I did try to look east but there was only grey mist and a bitter wind in my face so my cheeks felt as if they were being soldered to my sunglasses. There was time for one photo and then we beat a hurried retreat with faces to the ground and numb fingers. There was nothing triumphant about the undignified, stumbling descent from the snowcap; all we were trying to do was run away and hide from the tugging wind. My brain was too cold and oxygen-thirsty to register the moment, it just ached. The mountain shrugged us off.

We recovered and made tea at camp 2 and shook hands while our faces glowed. Mustafa called his friends in town who confirmed that the high winds were the beginning of the big storm. It would be best to get off the mountain soon. We packed up the stove and began the long descent.